A MAN WHO KNEW HOW
TO FORGIVE

A MAN WHO KNEW HOW TO FORGIVE

INCIDENTS FROM THE LIFE OF ST. JOSEMARÍA ESCRIVÁ

By Francesc Faus

 Scepter

Copyright © 2011, Scepter Publishers, Inc.
P.O. Box 211, New York, N.Y. 10018
www.scepterpublishers.org

Text design by Rose Design

Printed in the United States of America

ISBN: 978-1-59417-153-6

CONTENTS

INTRODUCTION

A man who'd suffered the loss of several family members killed by the militia during the Spanish Civil War was deeply troubled. Gripped by turbulent emotions, he decided to have a large roadside cross placed at the spot where they had died to recall the crime committed there. To him it seemed an act of justice to keep that atrocity from ever being forgotten.

When he spoke of his plan to a priest, he received disconcerting advice: "You shouldn't do it, because your motive is hatred. It would not be Christ's Cross, but the devil's."[1] The cross was never placed there, and the man learned how to forgive.

To forgive another person is one of the most difficult human acts. Injustice provokes a passionate reaction, and often it can seem that forgiving the other person would be a mistake—condoning an act of aggression or accepting an injury in a cowardly fashion. Forgiving someone also is hard because, far from indifference or coldness in the face of evil, it means suffering a real "wound" and then pardoning the other from one's heart. That may be why people sometimes say forgiving can be beyond human strength.

Yet to live without forgiving would be inhuman; a person who refuses to forgive hurts only himself in the end. But how

---

1. Andrés Vázquez de Prada, *The Founder of Opus Dei, Vol. II: God and Daring* (New York: Scepter Publishers, 2003), 278.

can we always forgive? How can we accept the past and bear with hurtful experiences? There are no easy answers. The path to forgiveness is never easy. Each of us must find his own way.

This book offers some stories of forgiveness from the life of the priest just mentioned, Josemaría Escrivá, the founder of Opus Dei. Canonized in 2002 by Pope John Paul II, he is a modern-day saint who made a lifelong effort to learn ever more perfectly the secret of forgiveness from the One who, nailed to a cross, prayed, "Father, forgive them for they know not what they do."[2]

The events related here are grouped in three periods of time: before, during, and after the Spanish Civil War. This conflict, the most important event of the twentieth century in the civil and political life of Spain, is considered by many historians to have been the opening phase in what would soon become the Second World War.

2. Lk 23:34.

PART I

FORGIVING AMID A CLIMATE OF HATRED

A YOUNG AND POOR STUDENT

Josemaría Escrivá was a young priest, twenty-nine years old, when in 1931 the lowering clouds of hatred and violence foreshadowed the imminent onset of what would become a catastrophic civil war.

In March 1925, at the age of twenty-three, he had been ordained a priest in Saragossa. In April 1927 he moved to Madrid with his widowed mother, Doña Dolores, and his sister and brother, Carmen and Santiago, to pursue a doctorate in law. In Madrid, while studying for his doctorate, he dedicated himself intensely to the service of the poor and abandoned in the outskirts of the city and the incurably sick in public hospitals. He also gave classes of Roman law and Canon law in the Cicuéndez Academy, which provided the small salary with which he tried to support his family. After his father's financial ruin and death, his family had experienced hard times, and often suffered real want.

There in Madrid on October 2, 1928, with social and political unrest already beginning to emerge, Josemaría had seen what his mission on earth was to be: opening up in the middle of the world a "path of holiness in professional work and in the fulfillment of the Christian's ordinary duties," as a prayer card asking for St. Josemaría's intercession puts it. This "path," later to become known as Opus Dei, offered a new ideal, which seemed revolutionary at the time: the possibility for any Christian to become holy in everyday life among the professional, family, and social relationships that make up most people's ordinary life.

To understand this "man who knew how to forgive" it will help briefly to sketch the atmosphere of hatred, intransigence, and violence, so opposed to reconciliation and forgiveness, oppressing Spain in the years immediately before the civil war and during the three years of that bloody conflict.

'DARKENING CLOUDS

In circles close to the far-right party of Fascist inspiration called the Falange, the conviction was growing that the only dialogue possible with the radical left—the socialists, anarchists, and communists, who were united by the coalitions of the government of the Republic—was "the dialectic of fists and guns."

At the same time, in the agitated ranks of the anarchists and the communists, still intoxicated by the recent victory of the Communist revolution in Russia in 1917, it was not unusual to hear someone say that Spain's problems would only be solved "on the day the last priest was strangled with the intestines of the last bishop."

The propaganda of the far left, emanating from the mixed coalition that formed the governing Popular Front, exacerbated the hatred and prejudice against religion. Hadn't Marx himself defined religion as the "opium of the people?" Wasn't Christianity being implacably persecuted in Russia? The Church and the clergy were seen as agents of reaction to be eliminated. Messianic and antagonistic ideologies, closed to any possibility of dialogue, were the order of the day.

The great majority of the population did not agree with these extreme ideologies. After free elections, a centrist coalition held power for a short time. But the Pandora's box of extremism had been opened, and the streets of Madrid, Barcelona, and other cities were already stained with the blood of the dead of both sides, while the "people's militias" left churches and convents in flames.[1]

---

1. See Stanley G. Payne and Javier Tussel, *La Guerra civil: Una nueva vision del conflicto que dividió España* (Madrid, 1966); Burnet Bolloten, *La Guerra civil española: Revolución y contrarrevolución* (Madrid, 1989).

On May 11, 1931, smoke from the burning of ten convents and monasteries darkened the sky of Madrid. Similar events took place the following day in many Spanish cities, and over a hundred monasteries and convents were set ablaze. The civil authorities proved helpless to contain the situation. In October 1934, an unsuccessful coup d'état in Asturias resulted in the destruction of 58 churches and the killing of 34 priests.[2]

The Popular Front government was relentlessly taken hostage by extremists whose eagerness to do away with religion and priests led to open persecution of Catholics. Thus Catholics had no alternative but to join, often unwillingly, the side opposed to the government of the Republic.

It is easy to imagine the heightened tensions and political fervor among young people and adults during those years. Josemaría Escrivá had begun to spread the Christian ideals of Opus Dei among university students and workers, but it was slow going and very few responded at first. When the war broke out, the members of Opus Dei numbered fewer than a dozen: all were young people, most of them students, at an age when passions are strongest.

Amid these polarizing currents, Josemaría Escrivá created around him an atmosphere of reconciliation and friendship, with respect for all social and political positions defensible by a Catholic, along with a serene understanding of those who held ideological views incompatible with or even aggressively opposed to Christianity. He thus made a reality in his own life the motto of St. Augustine: *Interficere errorem, diligere errantem.* "Fight error, but love the person who is in error." For Josemaría, fighting error meant knowing how to dialogue and

---

2. *Studia et Documenta—Rivista dell'Istituto Storico San Josemaría Escrivá,* Vol. 3 (Rome, 2009), 25ff; and Andrés Vázquez de Prada, op. cit. Vol. II, 11.

learning to listen with patience and respect to those who do not agree with oneself.

A HEART IN LOVE WITH FREEDOM

One of Escrivá's first followers, Pedro Casciaro, was the son of a staunch socialist, a prominent champion of the Republic, who after the civil war was persecuted by the Nationalists but managed to save his life by fleeing to Algiers. Pedro was studying mathematics and architecture in Madrid, and shared in almost all of St. Josemaría's adventures during the agitated years leading up to the war. His testimony, condensed in an exciting book, *Dream and Your Dreams Will Fall Short*,[3] is of great value.

He relates that the Father (as those close to St. Josemaría called him) "instilled us with serenity. His reflective, balanced attitude was in total contrast to the polarization all around us. He never discussed political matters. His judgments of events were always exclusively priestly ones. . . . He suffered a lot: for the Church and for the situation in his country, which he loved so much. He respected any opinion, related to public life, which a Christian could legitimately hold."

Among the few members of Opus Dei and the other young people Escrivá was guiding spiritually, Pedro Casciaro recalls, there was a great diversity of political views, and he "taught us to have a great respect for each person's freedom."[4]

One of those young men, Jose Luis Muzquiz, a recently graduated engineer, relates that some of them were curious to know where the Father's political sympathies lay: "I asked him

---

3. Pedro Casciaro, *Dream and Your Dreams Will Fall Short* (New York: Scepter Publishers, 1998).

4. Casciaro, 60–61.

what opinion he had about a very famous political figure at the time. He replied immediately: 'Look, nobody here will ask you about your political views. People from all sectors come here: Carlists, people from Popular Action, Spanish renewal monarchists. Yesterday, the President and Secretary of the Basque National Students' Association were here. On the other hand, you will be asked many other "awkward" questions. You will be asked if you pray, if you make good use of your time, if you keep your parents happy, if you study, because for a student studying is a serious obligation.' "[5]

Pedro Casciaro confirms these recollections. As the son of a prominent republican, who (as we will see below) like his father would suffer at the hands of the Nationalists, he was in a privileged position to do so. In a climate of "resentful reprisals . . . not once did I ever see or hear the Father say or do anything that was not in keeping with his serenity, prudence, and charity towards everyone. Of all of us who were closest to him then, maybe no one was as aware of this as I was, because of my complex family situation. I would immediately have detected a wounding comment, a contemptuous gesture or allusion. But he never made one. The Father never talked about politics. He wished for and prayed for peace and the freedom of consciences. Open to everybody, and with real greatness of heart, he longed for everyone to turn to God and get closer to him. . . . He never expressed resentment. In those days it was not easy to combine love of justice with charity; but the Father knew how to do it admirably."[6]

---

5. Hugo de Azevedo, *Uma Luz no Mundo*, ed. Prumo/Rei dos Livros (Lisbon, 1998), 78–79; and Casciaro, 61.

6. Casciaro, 115–116.

RECONCILIATION THROUGH SOCCER

A soccer match in Madrid's main prison owed its inspiration to Escrivá's determination to foster harmony among those who disagree politically.

Disturbances and skirmishes were becoming part of daily life; as a consequence, many overexcited adherents of divergent political tendencies were being rounded up by the police. One of these, who met Escrivá in the summer of 1932, gives this account.[7]

On the 10th of August in 1932 I took part in an attempted coup that failed only a few hours after it had begun. A colleague and I were arrested and incarcerated in the Modelo Prison in Madrid. Josemaría used to visit us often; he never showed the slightest vacillation, regardless of the risk, when it came to the spiritual care of people. To see him come dressed in a cassock was truly amazing, since wearing such garb at that time was very dangerous.

We would wait in the visiting room for political prisoners, a large hall with two grilles about ten centimeters apart that separated visitors and prisoners. There, through the grilles of that visitors' room, my attention was continually drawn to the spiritual tone of his conversations. He insisted on the importance of work and study, which at first seemed to me hardly appropriate, given the circumstances of our enforced imprisonment. But the way he spoke, making us suddenly realize the sanctifying value of work, produced an immediate effect. I began there and then to give classes and study French.

---

7. Hugo de Azevedo, 83. Testimony of Jose Manuel Doménech de Ibarra, in *Registro Histórico del Fundador*, RHF 872, and of Jose Antonio Palacios, RHF 2750.

During those months, some Anarchists from southern Spain (Cádiz, if I remember correctly) killed several civil guards, including the barracks chief, and proclaimed the 'libertarian revolution.' They also were arrested and locked up in the Modelo Prison, in a different section from ours. Each day all the prisoners (common prisoners as well as political) went out into different yards for exercise. We were dumbfounded when we saw Anarchists in our own yard. We usually played soccer, and continued to do so under the frightened gaze of these unexpected companions.

At the first opportunity, I explained my problem to the Father: "How can we be expected to get along with men who are so opposed to our own ideals and our faith?" His reply stopped me in my tracks: "Now you have the opportunity to speak with them, to converse with each one of them in particular, with respect and kindness. Keep in mind that they probably did not have Christian parents as you did, nor live in surroundings like yours. What would have become of you and me if we were in their situation? We shouldn't forget that we have received the faith gratuitously, and have the obligation to spread it. Now you have the opportunity on this playground to show that you are Christians, living and playing ball with them as if they were your best friends." And he added: "When you pray the *Our Father*, pay a lot of attention to the first two words: *Our . . . Father.*"

This person was stunned. But after thinking it over, he followed the advice. "After a few days of tense relations on this playground, a soccer match was organized along the terms suggested by the Father. I was the goalkeeper and my defensemen were two Anarchists. We never played the same position for long, but often changed places. I have never played soccer with greater style and less violence. On leaving prison, I kept up a friendship with some of them; and a number of them came back to the Church."

CLIMBING THE HILL OF FORGIVENESS

Stories like these might give the impression of Josemaría Escrivá de Balaguer as a person who was insensitive or unfeeling by nature. Before moving on, we need to correct that misconception.

In fact, the worth of his patience and forgiveness can only be appreciated if we take into account that his character was, by nature, just the opposite of cold or callous. Josemaría Escrivá, far from being a naturally easygoing man, had a strong, energetic temperament, prone to quick and passionate reactions. His ability to forgive can only be adequately explained by his struggle for self-dominion in the service of his mission, and above all, by his love—a love for God and men that aspired to become ever greater, vivified by the root from which it drew its strength: God's grace. This transformation took place without sacrificing the generous impulsiveness of his decisions and actions, the energy and forcefulness of his words and deeds.

As his biographer Andrés Vázquez de Prado says, documenting the statement with anecdotes and testimonies, "Throughout his life Josemaría had to struggle against the natural impetuosity of his temperament, to rein in that torrent of healthy energy and turn it into a controlled force and a strength of spirit with which to confront obstacles."[8]

---

8. Vázquez de Prada, Vol. I, 65.

No one is born virtuous and holy. Josemaría was a pleasant and likable child, but he had difficulty restraining himself when provoked. Let us consider three incidents from his youth.[9]

First, a fight that came to blows with a schoolmate who was mercilessly called "Pig Foot" because he went around with dirty knees. He insulted and struck the smaller Josemaría, who wouldn't tolerate it, and they ended up in a real brawl. Recalling the scrap, Josemaría said, "Whatever reason I might have had for doing what I did, I lost it the moment I took a swing at that companion of mine, because there is never any reason for anyone to resort to violence; it left me with a very bitter taste in my soul."[10]

The second incident occurred when Josemaría was a small child. Tired of repeatedly being served the same dish he didn't like, he got so angry that he threw the food against the wall. His Father quietly asked him to clean up the mess, but he waited several months before having the stain on the wallpaper removed as a visible reminder of the tantrum.[11]

A third incident from his youth. Born in 1902, Josemaría had four sisters. An affectionate child with a big heart, he saw three of them die, one after another. María del Rosario, only nine months old, died in 1910; then five-year old Lolita two years later; and finally María Asunción, only eight, died in 1913. A few months before this last death, Josemaría, deeply saddened, entered a room where his older sister Carmen, Maria Asunción, and a friend, María del Carmen, were making castles out of playing cards. As María del Carmen tells it, "We were just finishing a castle when Josemaría reached out with one

---

9. See Javier Echevarría, *Memoria del Beato Josemaría Escrivá* (Madrid: Rialp, 2000), 88; and Vázquez de Prada, Vol. I, 19 and 38.

10. Echevarría, 88.

11. See ibid., 88.

hand and knocked it over. We started crying and asked him, 'Why did you do that, Josemaría?' And he, in a very serious tone of voice, answered us, 'That's exactly what God does with people. You build a castle and, when it's almost finished, God knocks it over on you.'"[12]

Finally, an incident from 1923, while he was a prefect in the seminary, which left a bitter taste in Josemaría's soul. One day another seminarian, much older than Josemaría, a good person but rather coarse, insulted the younger man as he had done several times before. Losing his composure, Josemaría replied, and shoving and punching followed. According to the report by the seminary rector, which is still preserved, the other seminarian "had spoken to him in gross language, improper of a cleric, and in my presence had insulted him in the Cathedral of La Seo." And he adds that the way the seminarian Escrivá accepted the punishment given him by his superiors "was really a glory for him, since in my judgment it was his adversary who had struck first and most."

Even so, Josemaría lost his spiritual peace and felt a need to pour out his soul in a letter to his former spiritual director in the seminary of Logroño, Father Gregorio Fernández. On October 26 he received this reply: "I know the nobility of your sentiments, and I'm sure that by now you do not hold in your heart the slightest trace of resentment. . . . You should not discuss this matter with anyone other than God."

The episode ended on a positive note for everyone. After St. Josemaría's death, a letter from his old adversary was found among his papers. Dated October 8, 1952, it was written while the latter was a chaplain in a Red Cross hospital. After so many years, he magnanimously said: "Repentant, and in the most

---

12. Vázquez de Prada, Vol. I, 38.

humble and absolute way possible. *Mea culpa!*[13] It all seems to suggest that Josemaría was hardly at fault in resorting to violence, but he refused to excuse himself. He kept silent, prayed for his colleague, and never tried to justify himself. "Violence never," he repeated throughout his life. "It never helps to convince or win over anyone."

PREJUDICE AND CLASS HATRED

Now let's move on to the troubled years when the Spanish Civil War was drawing near. Awash in Marxist and anarchist propaganda, the proletariat was being summoned to revolution—in imitation of the Russian revolution—with the aim of ending oppression by the bourgeoisie and its allies, mainly the Church, according to persistent propaganda.

In the 1930s a priest could not walk on the streets of Madrid (and many other cities and towns) without being the target of insults and jibes. St. Josemaría, who wore a cassock right up to 1936, constantly took this abuse.

Four such incidents will serve to illustrate Josemaría's struggle to control his reaction, and to excuse and forgive.[14]

THE CONSTRUCTION WORKER COVERED WITH LIME

In 1930 the Father arrived at the Cicuéndez Academy, where he taught, with white splotches all over his cassock. The students were surprised since he always dressed neatly and cleanly. One of them, Mariano Trueba, asked him what had happened, then

---

13. Ibid., 127–128, and Echevarría, 73–74.
14. See Vázquez de Prada, Vol. I, 204, 272, 275.

later told the others. As was his custom, Josemaría was riding on the streetcar to the academy when a small group of construction workers noticed him. One of them, his overalls covered with lime, approached Josemaría meaning to get lime all over his cassock. Looking him in the eyes and realizing his intention, the priest gave him a big hug before he could react. "Come here, my son, coat me with as much of that stuff as you like! Are you pleased with the effect?" Mariano Trueba told his companions he thought Father Josemaría could only have done this if he was a saint.

BLACK SPAIN!

In 1931, Josemaría tells us in his *Intimate Notes*, "I was on Fernández de la Hoz Street, near Cisne, when I came across a group of bricklayers. One of them, in a mocking tone of voice, shouted, 'Black Spain!' The instant I heard that, I resolutely turned around and faced them. I remembered what Father [his confessor, Father Valentin Sanchez Ruiz] had said, and I spoke calmly, without anger. They all agreed that I was right, including the one who had done the shouting. He, and also another of them, shook hands with me."

A COCKROACH!

"Another incident," writes Josemaría in his *Intimate Notes*: "Lista Street, at the end of the street. This poor priest was coming back, tired, from his novena. A bricklayer turned aside from his work and said, insultingly, 'A cockroach! It should be stepped on!' Often I turn a deaf ear to such insults, but this time I could not. 'How courageous of you,' I said to him, 'picking on a gentleman who walks by you doing nothing to offend you! That's freedom?'

The others made him shut up, indicating, without openly saying so, that I was right. A few steps further on, another bricklayer tried to give me a reason for his colleague's conduct. 'It's not right,' he said, 'but you have to understand, he hates priests.' And he said it so matter-of-factly."

Josemaría was in the right here, yet he was unhappy with his reaction, as the following incident shows.

MUD ON HIS HEAD

This personal note is from the beginning of August 1931. "The barrage of insults against priests continues. . . . I made the resolution—I am renewing it—of keeping quiet when they insult me, even if they spit on me. One night, in Chamberí Plaza, when I was going to the Mirasol building, someone threw a fistful of mud at my head that almost plugged up my ear."

How did he react? "I didn't say a word. Even more: the resolution that I am talking about includes pelting those poor haters with Hail Mary's. I thought that my resolve was very strong, but the day before yesterday I failed twice, kicking up a fuss instead of being meek."

As we can see, he struggled, improved and prayed. He strove to learn to forgive. He had victories and also some unhappy defeats. But he wanted to learn to love, even while being hated. This is evident in what he wrote in his *Intimate Notes* a few weeks later, on September 18, 1931:

> I have to thank my God for a remarkable change. Until recently, the insults and taunts directed at me, as a priest, since the coming of the Republic (before that, they were very rare), made me furious. I decided that when I heard such vulgarities and obscenities, I would say to the Blessed Virgin a Hail Mary

for whoever uttered them. I have done that. It has cost me. But now, when I hear those ignoble words, they only make me feel, as a rule, deeply sorry for those poor, unfortunate people. For when they act in this way, they think they are doing something noble, since others, exploiting their ignorance and passions, have made them believe that, besides being a lazy parasite, the priest is an enemy—an accomplice of the bourgeoisie in exploiting them.[15]

FESTERING HATRED

And here is a postwar incident from the forties. It shows how, years after the armed conflict, the prejudices that had poured out during the previous decade still festered in people's hearts.

One day Josemaría had to take a taxi in Madrid. As usual, he began a conversation with the driver. He spoke about God in a friendly tone, about the beauty of sanctifying one's work, about friendship and a spirit of dialogue and understanding with everyone, including those with different viewpoints. The taxi driver listened without saying a word. When they reached their destination and the priest was about to get out, the driver finally said, "Listen, where were you during the time of the war?"

"In Madrid," the priest answered.

"Too bad they didn't kill you," the driver replied.

Josemaría was quick to forgive him. To show he didn't hold a grudge, he asked, "Do you have any children?" When the driver nodded, he gave him all the change in his pocket, saying, "Here, buy some candy for your wife and children."[16]

---

15. Ibid.
16. Ibid., Vol. II, 278.

WHERE DID THIS FORGIVENESS COME FROM?

Josemaría Escrivá carried on a constant interior struggle to forgive. Much more than just a determined effort to gain self-control, his ability to forgive had deeper sources. Before continuing, let's take a quick look at perhaps the most important.

On November 28, 1932, he recorded the following resolution in his *Intimate Notes*: "I will make an effort, if necessary, always to forgive those who offend me, from the very first moment. For no matter how great the injury or offense that has been done to me may have been, God has forgiven me more."[17]

Even an atheist or agnostic can appreciate that the ability to forgive is a sign of greatness of soul and a strong character. But it can also be compatible with arrogance and vanity. Only Christian humility enables a person to forgive without becoming proud.

Escrivá considered himself a sinner—"a sinner who loves Jesus Christ," as he often said. When he thought his faults showed a lack of correspondence to God's love, they weighed heavily on him. He spoke about this in a graphic way, at times with the humor of a man who knows how to laugh at himself:

"I have more 'faults' than a soccer match,"[18] he used to remark. On March 6, 1972, commenting on Christ's words that it is not the healthy that need a doctor but the sick,[19] he said: "This has been my constant prayer the whole day: 'Lord, here I am, a chronic sick person, and I need you!'"[20]

---

17. *The Way: Critical-Historical Edition* prepared by Pedro Rodriguez (London/New York: Scepter Publishers, 2009), 623. An adapted version of this note became no. 452 of *The Way*.

18. In Spanish, *faltas* means both "faults" and "fouls." Echevarría, 125.

19. Mk 2:17.

20. Echevarría, 20.

Knowing himself to be in constant need of God's mercy enabled him to be merciful toward others. As John Paul II said in his encyclical on divine mercy: "Man attains to the merciful love of God, his mercy, to the extent that he himself is interiorly transformed in the spirit of that love towards his neighbor."[21]

Awareness of being a sinner in need of forgiveness did not take away his peace or hope. He lived trustingly, because he abandoned himself to the mercy of God. "The Lord sustains me, because I am a sack of filth. I continually seek union with God, and he gives me a lot of peace and serenity."[22]

A WAGER BY HIS STUDENTS

But let's go back to the cassock dirtied with lime, since this story has a sequel. After hearing what had happened, the students at the Cicuéndez Academy were even more astonished when a teacher told them about a completely unknown dimension of Josemaría's life.

He said this young priest, an intellectual with a degree in law from the University of Saragossa and another in theology from the pontifical university of that city who was now pursuing a doctorate in law at the University of Madrid, devoted himself to caring for hundreds of poor and sick people in Madrid's slums and public hospitals. This, he added, was why Josemaría went from one end of Madrid to the other, spending hours and hours walking or on a streetcar.

Hardly able to believe it, the students decided to make bets on whether it was true. Following him secretly one day, they ended up at the northern edge of the city in the slums of Tetuan

21. *Dives in Misericordia*, no. 14, and *Catechism of the Catholic Church*, 2844.
22. Echevarría, 25.

de las Victorias; another day they followed him as he went south to the distant shanty-town of Vallecas.[23]

Escrivá was also very concerned about those who were morally "distant" and showed them great kindness. Whatever sacrifice it took, he was diligent in extending to them reconciliation with God and neighbor, and the balm of mercy.[24] Here are a few examples.

THE WOUNDED GYPSY

One day the Foundation for the Sick, where he served as chaplain, asked him to assist a gypsy who had been gravely wounded in a knife fight. Finding the man dying in a dirty hovel, he asked:

"How are you feeling?"

"Very bad, Father. Could you hear my confession?"

"Of course!"

After the confession, the priest, smiling warmly, encouraged him: "Jesus has forgiven you. Would you like to kiss the crucifix?"

Tears flowing down, the gypsy blurted, "How can I kiss our Lord with these putrid lips of mine?"

St. Josemaría replied, "But soon you'll be giving him a kiss in heaven; and what's more, you'll be getting a hug from him!"[25]

THE BROTHEL OWNER'S BROTHER

One day he received an unusual request. A woman who owned a brothel had a younger brother there who was gravely ill, in

---

23. Vázquez de Prada, Vol. I, 205.

24. Ibid., 325ff. and 338ff.

25. RHF 20770, p. 547.

danger of dying at any moment, and unable to be moved. The young man had asked for a priest, and his sister, a woman with faith—though lamentably far from practicing it—anxiously sought a solution. She had heard about a priest who was ready to go anywhere to help a soul, so she asked that he be called.

Josemaría was willing to assist her dying brother, but said he would go only if accompanied by a well-known and respected gentleman, well up in years, and on the condition that God would not be offended in that house that day. The owner agreed, and her brother died in God's peace, with the consolation of the sacraments, comforted by the priest's words of faith and hope.[26]

THE STRENGTH WITH WHICH TO GO FORWARD

The King's Hospital in Madrid was filled to overflowing with patients, with many lying in the corridors. Josemaría visited there frequently, often accompanied by young men enthused by his message of holiness and apostolate in the middle of the world. They would provide various services for the patients, almost all tubercular, bathing them, trimming their nails and hair, emptying bedpans, etc.

Among the dozens of terminal TB patients whom Escrivá ministered to (ignoring the risk of becoming infected himself) was a woman who, because of family and personal connections, had formerly occupied a very high social position but now was reduced to a wretched state. For years she'd lived a dissolute life, and in the end she was sick and abandoned by everyone. As her life drew to a close, divine Providence brought a priest to her who wasn't scandalized by her past and extended his consecrated hand to her to forgive and bless, just as Christ did with

---

26. Ibid., 20165, pp. 973–974, and 20590, p. 141.

the sinful woman in Simon's house and with the woman taken in adultery. He helped her to be reconciled with God, to receive lovingly the last sacraments, and to offer the pain she was suffering as expiation for her sins. The woman was very happy, with a peace so deep and serene that Josemaría would later say, "I was crazy with envy. . . . That woman was repeating, savoring the words, so happy: 'Blessed be pain!'" For pain, by purifying her, was opening to her the gates of heaven.[27]

Recalling those intense years spent among the poor and the sick, the abandoned and the wretched of Madrid, Josemaría said it was there, in those people whom society had marginalized, that he found the strength and solid ground for the founding of Opus Dei. He prayed for them and asked them to pray and offer their sufferings to God "for a work that will give much glory to God"—Opus Dei, which at the beginning didn't even have a name.[28]

"I went to seek strength in the poorest districts of Madrid. Hours and hours going everywhere, day after day, on foot from one place to another among the shamefully and wretchedly poor, so poor that they didn't have a thing to their name. . . . And in the hospitals: that King's Hospital in Madrid, full of consumptives at a time when consumption was incurable. Those were the weapons with which to fight and win! That was the strength with which to go forward!"[29]

27. See RHF 20590, p. 136.

28. Ibid., 20590, p. 136.

29. Salvador Bernal, *Msgr. Josemaría Escrivá, A Profile of the Founder of Opus Dei* (New York/London: Scepter Publishers, 1977), 178–179.

PART II ✸

FORGIVENESS IN TIMES
OF WAR

THE CONFLICT BREAKS OUT

The Spanish Civil War began on July 18, 1936, with a military uprising headed by several army generals, including Francisco Franco.

Passions already near the boiling point now erupted with unprecedented violence. In the first month of the war, cities and towns in the zone controlled by the government of the Republic witnessed many scenes of anticlerical fury. In August alone, 2,077 priests, friars, and nuns were assassinated—an average of 70 a day—in addition to the summary executions of many lay people for the mere fact of being Catholics.[1]

At the time, I was living in Barcelona, a city under the control of the Popular Front for the entire duration of the war and the scene of violent persecution of the Church. My personal knowledge of this persecution is minimal, since when the war broke out I was only four and half years old. But some events remain deeply impressed on my memory, and two in particular stand out.

I remember as if it were yesterday how my mother, very frightened, one day gathered up all the prayer books and religious objects in our home and spent the afternoon burning them in the building's furnace room. Even the wearing of a simple crucifix was now sufficient reason for the People's Militia to execute the guilty person with a bullet in the back of the neck or in the chest. "Armed groups felt authorized to search any house, and arrest the 'enemies of the people' and execute them. So any resentful individual could 'denounce' someone against whom he had a grudge."[2]

---

1. See Casciaro, 60–61.
2. Hugo de Azevedo, *Missão Cumprida* (Lisbon, 2008), 37.

My second recollection is this. After one of the worst bombing raids, my family left the city and walked a few miles to a farmhouse outside Barcelona that we rented for vacations. There we remained, safe from the bombs. One day a local farmer came by, dressed in a sombrero and cheap shoes and carrying a basket of vegetables. My father greeted him very cordially. Soon after we all gathered in my parents' room, where they had placed a glass, a piece of bread, and a bottle of wine on top of the chest of drawers. The "farmer" was a priest in disguise. Like so many others, he risked his life to supply the clandestine consolation of Mass once in a great while. At the beginning of this Mass, we children and my parents walked around the room several times, each of us carrying a small branch. Only years later did I realize that we had been celebrating Palm Sunday, and the circling around the room was the nearest thing to a liturgical procession we could manage. This was the only time in those three years that we could take part in a Mass.

By the end of the war, a good number of priests, especially Basque nationalists, had been killed by right-wing extremists. The remainder of the balance looked like this: 13 bishops assassinated by communists and anarchists (among them, the bishop of Barbastro, Escrivá de Balaguer's hometown, who was publicly castrated and then dragged, naked and bleeding, through the streets of the city), 4,184 diocesan priests, 2,365 religious, friars and members of religious institutes, and 283 nuns.[3] The number of Catholic laity murdered is impossible to count. Several hundred priests, religious, and laypeople have been canonized in recent years as martyrs.

In Madrid, Josemaría Escrivá found himself at the center of all this hatred. Hugo de Azevedo writes: "Madrid was a hell

---

3. Antonio Montero, *Historia de la Persecución Religiosa en España*, 1936–1939 (Madrid, 1961), 728.

of hatred and death. The city was divided into predators and fugitives. But it was impossible to escape. That beautiful capital city had become an enormous prison where no one knew what would happen next. Bodies rotted in the streets or were left lying in the city squares for relatives to retrieve."[4]

PURSUED LIKE A CRIMINAL

On Monday July 20, 1936, Escrivá celebrated Holy Mass in the student residence at 16 Ferraz Street, then the only center of Opus Dei. Its two apartments were a residence for a few students where many other young people also came to study and to receive Christian formation. A few weeks before, the move from a previous center to this house had been completed at the cost of much sacrifice. Father Escrivá could not know that this Mass would be the last he would celebrate for some time.

To be a priest was now tantamount to wearing a sign saying "condemned to death." When the uprising by troops of the army garrison in Spanish Morocco led by Franco broke out, supporters of the Republican government immediately reacted with unheard-of viciousness against anyone suspected of conspiring with the organizers of the coup. This was especially so for any member of the military suspected of having "rightist" views and anyone who was or looked like a priest. No distinctions were made. "Priest" was synonymous with "enemy," to be eliminated as soon as possible.

St. Josemaría later painfully recalled: "Neither before nor after 1936 have I taken part either directly or indirectly in politics. If I had to hide out, pursued like a criminal, it has only been for professing my faith, even though our Lord did not consider

---

4. de Azevedo, *Missão Cumprida*, 37.

me worthy of the palm of martyrdom. On one of those occasions, in front of the house where we were living, they hanged a man they had mistaken for me."[5] He never learned this man's identity. "I know for a fact," says Bishop Javier Echevarría, St. Josemaría's secretary for many years and the current prelate of Opus Dei, "that he prayed for that person throughout the rest of his life, while begging our Lord's forgiveness for those who committed the murder."[6]

Hiding out, pursued like a criminal: that was his day-by-day existence in Madrid, from July 18, 1936 until October, 1937. Dressed as a layman, he went from hiding place to hiding place. He wore his deceased father's wedding ring, which his mother had given him so that people would take him for a married man. Often in danger of being arrested, he never ceased to exercise his priesthood in a clandestine way. He risked his life to carry out his priestly ministry and to bring spiritual comfort to members of Opus Dei in prisons, in hiding places, or on battlefronts. But this book is not meant to be a detailed account of those adventures. Here I speak of just a few events in which his spirit of forgiveness is manifest.

THE REFUGEES

He took refuge briefly in the homes of generous friends terrified at having a priest with them. Then two young doctors, friends and followers of Escrivá, convinced Dr. Angel Suils, a former schoolmate of his, to accept him as a patient in his psychiatric clinic on the outskirts of Madrid.[7] On October 7 a service

---

5. Vázquez de Prada, Vol. II, 109.

6. Ibid.

7. Ibid., 34ff.

vehicle from the Emergency Hospital, driven by a militiaman, went to pick up a "non-dangerous madman." On the way to the sanatorium, the driver remarked, "If he's that crazy, we might as well just shoot him and not waste our time."

Posing as a madman, he stayed at the clinic until mid-March 1937. He had to avoid the nurses who belonged to extremist trade unions and were soon suspicious of him. He knew that most of the patients were Catholics and would want to go to confession and receive Holy Communion. So, despite the danger, he made Dr. Suils promise that he would not allow any patient near death to die without receiving the last sacraments.

An incident of forgiveness during this period is as follows. When Josemaría decided to leave the sanatorium for another shelter, the doctor okayed his leaving, with a false diagnosis to justify his internment. The document read: "I certify that Jose María Escribá (*sic*) Albás, 35 years of age, has been treated by me since the age of 29 for an endogenous psychosis, which affects him periodically. He is discharged as of this day, having recovered from the latest outbreak of this illness, which required him to be interned in this sanatorium for several months, given the difficulties of treating him at home under the present circumstances. From today, we are allowing him to live with his sister."

After the war, in the city of Vitoria, he met a well-known priest who had been rector of the seminary of Madrid and before the war had publicly described Josemaría as a "crazy" visionary. Smiling, he approached this priest and showed him the certificate from Dr. Suils as if to say, jokingly, "You were right." Rather than rub it in, he chose to play down the old misunderstanding with a joke. The other priest, a good and zealous man, was so impressed that from then on he showed St. Josemaría constant and sincere affection.[8]

Again we are reminded of the deep roots of his ability to forgive. Alvaro del Portillo recounts a postwar incident: "At the beginning of the forties, an aunt of mine and her husband invited our Founder and me to a luncheon. Another guest was Manuel Aznar, a very well-known intellectual who was considered to be the best Spanish journalist of his day and would later become the Spanish ambassador to the United States. At one point this gentleman said to the Father, 'I would love to write your biography!' And the Father responded, 'Well, for me, one word is all that's needed: Sinner! But a sinner who loves Jesus Christ very much.'"[9] In pardoning others so readily, he was deeply aware of the pardon he constantly received from God. Often he spoke at having the "vocation of a prodigal son."

LIVING SPACE

On March 14, 1937, he left the sanatorium to take refuge in the Honduran consulate at 51 Paseo de la Castellana, the main avenue in Madrid's city center.[10] At the urging of family friends, Consul Pedro Jaime de Matheu Salazar welcomed him into that diplomatic refuge along with his brother Santiago and four members of Opus Dei.

They camped out in the living room for lack of any other space. Only in May were they able to move into a small room, apparently previously used for coal storage. It was so narrow that

---

8. de Azevedo, *Uma Luz no Mundo*, 145.

9. *Immersed in God* (interview with Alvaro del Portillo by Cesare Cavalleri) (New York: Scepter Publishers, 1996), 172.

10. Vázquez de Prada, Vol. II, 42 and ff.

when the mattresses they slept on were unrolled at night, the floor was completely covered. There was only one high, narrow window overlooking an interior space. During the day it was so dark they had to leave on the single bulb hanging from the ceiling.[11]

They remained in virtual exile in this diplomatic asylum for half a year, until August 1937. Hunger was a constant presence, along with uncertainty. Shortly before their arrival, the consulate of Peru had been invaded by the armed forces and the refugees hiding there— 300 Spaniards and 60 Peruvians— were arrested.

The consul's daughter, Consuelo, later recalled, "People were afraid; after my father told him it was dangerous to celebrate Mass in the foyer, he always celebrated it in their room."[12] The altar was an empty bottle box, turned upside down. The chalice was a drinking glass, given by the consul's wife.

Food was scarce and people went hungry. When Doña Dolores, Josemaría's mother, managed to visit him, she did not recognize him at first because he had become so thin. Only when he said "Mamá" did she recognize his voice and hug him, overcome with emotion.

FAMILY LIFE

With nerves at the breaking point, the refugees in the consulate were understandably inclined to complain all the time, venting their anger about the war and its calamities and anxious about delays in their hoped-for liberation. They also quarreled among themselves. But the little Opus Dei family managed to live in an atmosphere of work and serenity, cordiality and hope, which the other refugees noticed and even tried to imitate.

---

11. Ibid., 62.
12. Ibid., 64.

Josemaría encouraged his companions to organize their day as if nothing were out of the ordinary. He reminded them of the need to make good use of the "treasure" of time and to avoid useless daydreaming that gave free reign to the imagination. They therefore drew up a study schedule, including studying languages in anticipation of the future expansion of Opus Dei throughout the world. Time was set aside for material jobs and for growth in the spiritual life: prayer, Mass, Rosary, reading of the New Testament or some spiritual book. The Father preached a meditation to them almost every day, usually on the Gospel.[13] When possible they also tried to speak with the other refugees, encouraging them and seeking to bring them closer to God.

The consul's son-in-law, José Luis Rodríguez-Candela, afterwards remarked that he never saw in Josemaría "any sign of anxiety or depression. He was a person who made living together easy and pleasant. He never created problems of any kind, or made any comment that was less than positive—not about the red government, not about the white government, not about the bombings, not about any of the difficulties."[14]

One of the young fellows with him, Eduardo Alastrué, wrote: "Sometimes we thought: if only this could last forever! Had we ever known anything better than the light and warmth of that little room? As absurd as it was in those circumstances, that was our reaction, and from our way of seeing things it made perfect sense. It brought us peace and happiness day after day."[15]

Like Josemaría, all the refugees were fleeing unjust persecution that endangered their lives and families, their material possessions and livelihood. They had plenty of reasons to

---

13. Ibid.
14. Ibid., 77.
15. Ibid., 68.

deeply resent their persecutors. But it wasn't like that around the Father. With his great faith, he managed to communicate to those near him a deep spirit of understanding and forgiveness for everyone.

A NOTICEABLE ABSENCE

Vázquez de Prada remarks that although we normally notice some odd gesture or unusual word, things sometimes are noticed precisely because they are absent and *not* observed.[16] He makes this point in relation to the numerous letters Josemaría wrote during this enforced enclosure, some to his spiritual children who were not in the consulate and some to his own family. He wrote in code, sending the letters by means of couriers or various subterfuges. In that way he helped by letter those he could not help in person.

His biographer notes that something is missing from these letters that one might reasonably expect to find. "There are no references to or commentaries on political affairs. There is not a word about governments, zones, battlefronts, cities liberated or occupied, allies or enemies, victims or guilty parties. These silences are not because of censorship but for reasons of a spiritual nature, as indeed can be noticed in the remarks made by those who shared his consulate asylum. This approach meant that his sons did not develop any bellicose attitudes. In his presence, no one mentioned any military operations or crimes. One simply forgave and forgot."

But, Vázquez de Prada admits, "when necessary, the founder did touch on the subject of the war, and always referred to it as a catastrophe, but his priestly spirit was open to souls in both

---

16. Ibid.

zones and all factions. His general intercession at Mass took in the whole ocean of human suffering produced by the conflict—all the suffering at the battlefronts, in prisons, hospitals, homes, places of refuge. Father Josemaría's attitude was not one of lofty indifferences, but rather of consummate charity, stemming from a higher, supernatural vision of world events. 'He was always very concerned with what was happening,' says the consul's son-in-law, 'though at the same time he was very much above it. . . . He never spoke with hatred or rancor or judged anyone. On the contrary, he was always saying: *this is a barbarity, a tragedy.* He was saddened by what was happening, but not in a merely human way. When the rest of us celebrated victories, he remained silent.'"[17]

Here he was practicing what he preached: "Never think badly of anyone, not even if the words or conduct of the person in question give you good grounds for doing so."[18] "I don't want to put labels on anyone,"[19] he used to say. He knew that in each human being there is an abyss whose depths only God can fathom, a universe infinitely greater and richer than a person's errors and deficiencies might lead one to suppose.

Eduardo Alastrué, who spent those months alongside St. Josemaría, had a very good memory and took shorthand rapidly. Thanks to him, almost complete texts have survived of more than fifty meditations St. Josemaría preached during the six months in the Honduran consulate. As mentioned, the Father would gather his five companions—a number that later increased—to spend some time in prayer. To guide their prayer, he addressed reflections to them in a meditation composed

---

17. Ibid.

18. St. Josemaría Escrivá, *The Way* (New York: Scepter Publishers, 2008), no. 442.

19. Echevarría, 129.

partly of spiritual commentary and partly of direct dialogue with God.

The following extracts illustrate Escrivá's spirit of forgiveness during wartime.[20]

"The revolution," he said on August 24, "caught us by surprise, absorbed in our work, solely concerned with the desire to serve God. . . . If we remain faithful, won't God prepare a fruitful future for us, and all the more so if the harvest has been fertilized by our sufferings? . . . Thus, believing and hoping in Him, loving Him with all our strength, we will be happy and filled with peace, no matter what circumstances surround us. We will not lack joy, even in the midst of hunger, and disdain, and the loss of our freedom. I must confess that I've suffered horribly here. But I have to say as well that I've experienced deep joy in this confinement of ours. . . . Let us make the specific resolution today not to become angry or upset about anything, no matter what happens."

May 30: "How can we be harsh towards others when He isn't? His justice blends with his mercy, and produces a marvelous equilibrium, a gift we should implore for ourselves."

July 20: "Instead of quickly judging our neighbor, and perhaps harshly condemning him, we should consider what would have become of us if we had been placed in the environment of the person whom we've judged; if we had read the books that he read; if we had felt the passions that overpowered him. This consideration will help us show charity towards him. . . . Isn't Paul's example sufficient for us? Called to the apostolate at a late hour, he won so many souls for God; after being a persecutor of Christians, he became an example for everyone. Let's

---

20. Testimonial account *ad futuram memoriam* by Eduardo Alastrué Castillo, in AGP (General Archives of the Prelature).

be understanding then. Who knows whether that person, who perhaps we interiorly scorn and condemn, if corrected and purified and converted into a healthy stalk, might not produce more savory fruit than us?"

April 10: "Lord of mercy, grant me the grace to be merciful towards others. May I be unyielding with myself, while showing understanding to those around me. May I not judge others, so as not to be judged myself."

August 24: "We've tried hard to get out of this place but so far haven't managed to do so; all of our attempts have come to nought, one after another. How should we react? By not losing our peace. We should continue to use all the available means and trustingly place our hope in God. Faced with this situation, do we become angry, or give in to impatience or ill-humor? Why? Don't we deserve these setbacks in punishment for our sins and weaknesses? But You, Lord, don't punish anyone. You only know how to love."

THE FUGITIVE

"We've tried hard to get out of this place but so far haven't managed to do so." That was said in August—and before the month was out, he finally could leave. The "solution," a poor one and far from permanent, was a document signed by the consul designating him *Intendente* or Chief Supply Officer for that diplomatic legation (a certificate "falser than Judas," St. Josemaría said).

This was the first of many steps that would eventually carry him across the Catalonian and Andorran Pyrenees to his desired destination: the zone where the practice of religion was respected and priestly work could be done (except for those priests and lay people who had been allied with the "reds" and were now in prison). From Burgos, capital city of that part of

Spain, he would be able to give himself freely to the mission God had called him to.

It is beyond the scope of this book to describe all the stages of this journey with its many exciting events.[21] Escrivá's escape from the communist zone included a dangerous trip from Madrid to Barcelona, where he was reunited with some young members of the Work and friends (including Pedro Casciaro, Francisco Botella, Miguel Fisac, Juan Jiménez Vargas, José María Albareda, Manuel Sainz de los Terreros, and Tomás Alvira). From Bareclona they had to cross the Pyrenees, closely patrolled by Republican troops, in harsh winter weather (November–December 1937).

After many close escapes and adventures, they reached Andorra. From there they crossed over to France, arriving exhausted with tattered shoes and clothing totally inadequate for the snow and icy winds they had to face. After a short stop in Lourdes, they re-crossed the Pyrenees and entered the part of Spain under the control of the forces opposing the Republican government. After staying briefly in Pamplona, Father Josemaría was able to take up residence in January 1938 in a small hotel, the Sabadell, in Burgos. This would serve as the base for his apostolic operations, including tiring trips to those who needed his advice and friendly words.

MURDERED FRIENDS

The Father reached Pamplona on December 17, 1937, and there his priestly life gradually returned to normal. He also began to receive sad news about priest friends who had been assassinated. Even before the war, Father José María Somoano, the first priest to join St. Josemaría in Opus Dei, had been poisoned. Now

---

21. See Vázquez de Prada, Vol. II, 121–169; Azevedo, *Uma luz* . . . , 122–137.

he learned that one of his closest friends, Father Pedro Poveda (canonized by Pope John Paul II), founder of the Teresian Association active in the field of education, had been shot. Father Lino Vea-Murguía, arrested on August 16, 1937, was murdered and his body dumped by the wall of Madrid's East Cemetery. Another priest who had been Escrivá's baptismal godfather was also assassinated.

Years later, responding to a question from a woman who had suffered a very cruel persecution in her own country, he referred to some of these events. He recalled that his baptismal godfather, Don Mariano, "was a widower who later became a priest. They martyred him when he was sixty-three years old. I am called Mariano on his account. And the nun who taught me how to read and write at school, and who was a friend of my mother's before becoming a nun, was murdered in Valencia. All this doesn't horrify me, but it fills my heart with tears. For those people were mistaken; they didn't know how to love. I have recalled all this in order to console you, my daughter, not to speak about politics, because I know nothing about politics. I don't talk about it, nor will I ever do so as long as God leaves me in this world, since that's not my job. But tell your family, on my part, to join you and me in forgiving."[22]

During the war and after, when so many wounds festered with resentment, Josemaría spoke only of forgiving. He was well aware that resentment withers the heart and renders love sterile.

On one of his trips from Burgos, in April 1938, Father Josemaría met a young officer on the train. In a letter to his sons in Burgos, written from Cordoba, he wrote: "A second lieutenant, who had suffered tremendous harm to his family and his estate at the hands of the Reds, said that he would soon get his

---

22. Casciaro, 116–117.

vengeance. I told him that I too have suffered but that I want the Reds to be converted. These Christian words had a strong effect on his noble soul, consumed with a desire for violence, and he became quite thoughtful."[23]

THE PERISCOPE AND THE LAUGH

In the middle of the war, on June 7, 1938, Josemaría had the opportunity to go to the front lines outside Madrid, then seemingly frozen in place. One of the first members of Opus Dei, Ricardo Fernández Vallespín, an architect, had been injured when a defective grenade exploded near where he was working. Confined to a military hospital, he managed to send a telegram to the Father, telling him what had happened.

As soon as he could, the priest went to see the injured man. He spent the night in the command post of an artillery battery in Carabanchel Alto. The next day, looking through the unit's periscope, he could see the house at 16 Ferraz Street (the center of Opus Dei in Madrid, newly acquired in 1936). It was almost completely destroyed. He burst out laughing. An officer asked him why. "Because I'm looking at what little remains of my own house."[24]

St. Josemaría began laughed out of trust in God and hope for the future. It did not occur to him to speak badly of "enemies." The thorns of bitterness found no place in his heart.

A STORY OF RESENTMENT

Toward the end of June 1938, with the war raging, Pedro Casciaro was walking in Burgos when he encountered a woman

---

23. Vázquez de Prada, Vol. II, 277–278.
24. Bernal, 237–238.

who, seeing him, reacted with hostility. She looked at him in anger, as though seeing the very devil himself.

Pedro recognized her as the wife of a civil servant in the Treasury, Jorge Bermúdez, who before the war had lived in the same city as himself, Albacete, in a house near Pedro's family home. Bermúdez had a reputation as extremely right-wing.

Perplexed, Pedro racked his memory for some reason to explain such a reaction on the wife's part, but he could find none. When he arrived at the Sabadell Hotel where the Father was living, the latter informed him that he had just received word that Pedro had been denounced as an enemy of the regime by Mr. Bermúdez. An accusation like that could have very serious consequences. He had accused Pedro of being a communist, son of a leftist to whom crimes had been (falsely) attributed, and said he, Pedro, was a spy in General Orgaz's headquarters. This was reason enough for the firing squad or a lengthy prison term. The Father advised Pedro to visit the woman to try to clear up the misunderstanding and ask her to persuade her husband to withdraw the accusation.

"This visit," Pedro writes, "was counter-productive. . . . Among other things, she said it was unjust that while her son was risking his life at the front, I was peacefully in the rear, spying for the reds!" She refused to budge.

St. Josemaría decided to take the initiative and presented himself in the office of the Treasury where Mr. Bermúdez worked. The interview was very tense. Mr. Bermúdez was cold and insolent. The Father defended Pedro with paternal affection, declaring himself to be a trustworthy witness who had known Pedro several years. Remaining entirely calm, he tried to make Bermudez understand the injustice he was about to commit. But neither the earnest requests of the Father, full of charity, nor his strong words about justice succeeded in softening the heart of this poor man, who obstinately repeated that, if they couldn't apprehend the father, the son would have to pay the price for him. "Both the father and the son have to pay for this!"

Josemaría left the office saddened. He broke his silence only to say unexpectedly, as though moved by some ineffable inspiration, "Tomorrow or the day after, a funeral."

A few hours later they heard that Bermúdez had died suddenly in his office. Pedro recalled: "The sad news had a great impact on me. I fell ill and had to lie down in bed. Meanwhile the Father helped me to regain my composure and quietly told me to be at peace regarding that man, because he was morally sure God would have mercy on his soul and had given him the grace of final repentance. He added that since leaving his office he had not ceased praying both for him and for his children. . . .

"From that day forward, all my life I have prayed for his soul and for his family. I am sure he enjoys the glory of God thanks to divine mercy and the Father's prayers.

"God will have rewarded him for all his good works and will no doubt have forgiven him for those moments of darkness so understandable in the midst of war's chaos."[25]

There is a key to Josemaría Escrivá's readiness to forgive in something he wrote in his *Intimate Notes* on December 30, 1933: "If you have so many defects, why are you surprised to find defects in others?"[26] The heart of someone who sees himself as a sinner and in need of forgiveness is open to being understanding toward the weaknesses of others. Humility is fertile soil for understanding.

St. Josemaría was never scandalized by anyone. "All right: that person has behaved badly toward you. But, haven't you behaved

---

25. Casciaro, 139–144.

26. *The Way*, no. 442.

worse toward God?"[27] For "if God, despite my great personal wretchedness, treats me with confidence, I should therefore do the same with all souls."[28] Christ taught: *For if you forgive men their trespasses, your heavenly Father also will forgive you.*[29]

FORGIVENESS IN LESS DRAMATIC SITUATIONS: PATIENCE

We have been considering St. Josemaría's forgiveness in dramatic times and crisis situations. We can also find it at work in everyday settings, and consider, perhaps with a smile, what forgiveness is like among people who love each other but occasionally show their limitations and imperfections. Three incidents in Burgos combine affection and youthful thoughtlessness with a somewhat excessive audacity.

The setting was the Sabadell Hotel. The protagonists are Pedro Casciaro and Paco (Francisco) Botella, both mathematics students at the university. They had accompanied the Father on the dangerous journey across the Pyrenees and, along with José María Albareda, spent the most time with him in that small hotel.

A cassock gets badly torn

After crossing the Pyrenees, the Father and his sons didn't have a cent. To be exact, they had barely enough to pay the rent and buy the minimum needed to stay alive.

The Father, who set himself the goal of a very demanding practice of poverty based on the Gospel, therefore refrained

---

27. Ibid., no. 686.

28. Echevarría, 150.

29. Mt 6:14.

from spending money on any personal items, even though others might have considered them necessary.

These were the circumstances in which Pedro and Paco committed their gaffe in the matter of the Father's only cassock. It was an old cassock, given to him in Pamplona shortly after the crossing of the Pyrenees. It had become discolored, had tears in several places, and bore the signs of constant mending and stitching. Pedro and Paco kept asking him to have a new one made. The Father did not think that necessary and continued to use the old one.

One day Josemaría left the cassock lying in the room. The two decided to take action. "Paco and I," Pedro explains, "ripped the cassock down the back, where it was already very worn. We did not foresee the outcome. When he realized what we had done, he did not say a word. When we got back from the barracks we were ashamed to find the Father patiently sewing the cassock together again. We had failed completely. . . . Our failure was aggravated by the fact that the mend had not turned out very well and the Father now had to wear his cloak every time he went out. This was during the hottest part of the Burgos summer.

"In spite of everything, I am sure that deep down the Father was grateful for our actions. He really understood the mentality and the way of being of young people: and Paco and I were very young. When he saw us laughing at something nonsensical he would say: '*How fortunate you are!*'"[30] This, Pedro later remarked, was a kind way of saying that sometimes they were a pair of simpletons with their heads in the clouds.

How a glass got broken

Like all the saints, St. Josemaría felt a great need to be demanding on himself in practicing penance, in order to obtain from God

---

30. Casciaro, 138.

the graces to remain faithful to his vocation and advance the apostolic work of Opus Dei.

He practiced rigorous fasts, which distressed those who lived with him in Burgos. For example, he would say he had already eaten, and later they would discover that he'd bought some peanuts to "fool" his hunger. The same thing was true of drinking. Some days he would take only the small quantity of water used at the end of Mass to purify the chalice. Paco kept Pedro informed every night: " 'I don't think he has had any water today either.' We could even notice it, because when he spoke his mouth and throat would be dry. Days passed in the same manner until one night I filled a glass with water and I gave it to him commanding, 'Drink it!' "

"The Father refused and said I was overstepping my bounds. Then, only barely keeping my temper, I snapped back, 'Either you drink it or I drop it.' When I saw he would not give in, I dropped the glass on the floor and it smashed into smithereens. Amused and mimicking my tone, the Father said patiently, 'Temper!' The upshot was that I apologized, and Paco and I picked up the glass from the floor. A little while later he said affectionately, 'Be careful, don't walk around barefoot, there might be some splinters of glass on the floor.' "[31]

Years later, Pedro smilingly recall the Father's affectionate patience. "Once I heard him sighing, 'Poor man! Poor man!' I was curious and I asked him, 'Who are you referring to, Father?' 'Your father, my son, who else?' he replied, with that loving sense of humor so particularly his own. 'Your father must have been a saint to put up with you! And he left me the job of taming you!' "[32]

---

31. Ibid., 132.
32. Ibid., 130–131.

No chocolate or 'churros' left

The Father's companions in Burgos saw him receive all sorts of visitors: young men and old, lay people and priests, who came for his advice and spiritual direction. He usually received them in a little enclosed balcony that could be separated from the rest of the apartment by a curtain. Since the balcony was the only room's source of natural light, Paco and Pedro would say "Good night!" to each other whenever the curtain was drawn.

Despite the severe lack of money and the imperative need to save, the Father tried always to greet his visitors hospitably. "I remember," Pedro recalled, "one particularly telling event. He had invited a young fellow for breakfast, and we had hot chocolate with *churros* [a sweet roll often dipped in the thick chocolate]. When he had gone, we complained to the Father that his guest had really a good appetite, for he had gulped down several cups of hot chocolate one after the other and several helpings of *churros*." The others ended up fasting.

"The Father charitably and cheerfully made an excuse for him, as he always did. The problem, he said, was that the poor fellow had not managed to get his calculations right. He had finished a *churro* while he still had some hot chocolate left, and the hot chocolate was downed when he still had some *churros* left, and therefore he needed to keep replenishing his supply of one or the other. . . . He always knew how to put a sympathetic slant on any comment which might be, or seem to be, critical even though it was only meant as a joke or referred to something quite unimportant, as in this case."[33]

---

33. Ibid., 130.

PART III ❈

FORGIVENESS IN PEACETIME

"FRIENDLY FIRE"

In wartime soldiers occasionally encounter "friendly fire" coming from their own side.

The lives of saints have hardly ever been without friendly fire—misunderstanding, even persecution, by their brothers in the faith. This was a painful experience for St. John Chrysostom (attacked by, among others, St. Jerome, badly informed by Bishop Theophilos of Alexandria), St. Francis of Assisi (disowned by his own father), St. Teresa of Avila and St. John of the Cross (opposed by practically the entire Carmelite order), St. Ignatius of Loyola (the victim of envy and calumny), St. Pius of Pietrelcina, known as Padre Pio (denounced by a distinguished colleague and by the local bishop), and St. Paulina of Brazil (deposed from her position and silenced, confined to a convent by that good man Father Duarte Leopoldo y Silva, himself later a victim of baseless gossip).

In these cases the friendly fire wasn't directed at its targets by mistake, as in wartime, but consciously and deliberately. The detractors, laboring under a misconception, acted as they did because they were blinded (at least for a time) by mistaken notions about the facts and the intentions of those they opposed.

St. Josemaría Escrivá had his share of friendly fire. It supplied many opportunities for forgiveness which, refined under prolonged persecution, in the end became truly heroic.

THE CIRCUMSTANCES OF THE TIME

First, let's review briefly the historical circumstances in which these misunderstandings about St. Josemaría and Opus Dei arose.

Catholic reconstruction in the post-civil war era

Spain had just emerged from a brutal civil war that afflicted the country for three years. During the war, as we have seen, many Catholics, especially priests and religious, lived in constant fear for their lives. They had seen their churches burned and profaned, their schools converted into hospitals or barracks. When it became possible in Spain to practice religion again, many people felt great happiness and fervor. But many also felt a special sensitivity toward anything that, reasonably or not, might seem contrary to the Catholic faith and the Church's unity.

During that period of fervent reconstruction, it was also understandable that, even inadvertently, a certain competitive spirit should arise that led to rivalries and jealousy among brothers in the faith. Jealousy can warp the outlook of even very good people.

The situation of Opus Dei when the "friendly fire" broke out

Republican Madrid surrendered to the Nationalist forces on March 28, 1939. St. Josemaría was anxious to return to the capital to see his mother and brother and sister, as well as members of Opus Dei and friends. Also he wanted to visit the little that remained of the student residence at 16 Ferraz Street.

Wearing a cassock, he hitched a ride on a supply truck, and was one of the first to enter Madrid on the morning of March 29. After briefly greeting his family and close friends, he went to 16 Ferraz Street. There he found only partly destroyed walls and a heap of rubble.

He returned with some others on April 21 to see what they could salvage from the ruins. But all they found was a piece of imitation parchment that before the war had been framed and hung in the study room. It carried Christ's new commandment: *Love one another; even as I have loved you, that you also love one another. By this all men will know that you are my disciples, if you have love for one another.*[1]

So they had to start over almost from scratch and began looking for a new home to replace the one destroyed. Finally, on July 1, they managed to rent two apartments in a building at no. 6 Jenner Street. Two months later, in September, to the Father's great joy, they inaugurated the oratory of a new student residence.

A decorative feature of this oratory was a wooden frieze near the ceiling, which the students decorated with two Latin phrases. One was from the Acts of the Apostles: *Erant perseverantes in doctrina Apostolorum, et communicatione fractionis panis, et orationibus* ("They devoted themselves to the apostles' teaching and fellowship, to the breaking of bread and the prayers").[2] The other was from the ancient Eucharistic hymn, *Ubi Caritas: Congregavit nos in unum Christi amor* ("The love of Christ has gathered us into one").

The spaces between the Latin words contained classic motifs from Christian art, some dating from the time of the catacombs: crosses, a basket of bread and grapes (symbols of the Eucharist), and a dove (the Gospel symbol of the Holy Spirit).

There, in the intimacy of that little chapel, St. Josemaría began celebrating Mass and once again preaching to the students. The oratory was also available to the young men for personal meditation and adoration of the Blessed Sacrament. The residence was open without distinction to all for study, work sessions, musical or cultural get-togethers, the writing of doctoral theses, etc.

But the peaceful atmosphere didn't last long. Quite unexpectedly, the student residence became the object of calumny and

---

1. Jn 13:34–35.
2. Acts 2:42.

persecution. The story is an unpleasant one, but we must take a look at it for the sake of examining the topic of forgiveness.

The first thorns

The "opposition by the good," as St. Josemaría called it, began in Madrid in 1940. It soon spread to the rest of Spain, then to Rome, and eventually to many other parts of the world.

A warm atmosphere of fraternity existed in the new student residence at 6 Jenner Street. Many students would go there to study or attend activities of Christian formation, many apostolic projects and outreach programs for the needy were underway, and many people came seeking advice from Father Josemaría.

But in less than six months the extraordinary rumors began to circulate.[3] It was said, for example, that the oratory of the residence was full of cabalistic symbols and hieroglyphics (i.e., the Christian symbols on the wooden frieze mentioned above). Outside the oratory a simple wooden cross without the figure of Christ crucified had been placed on the wall, and it was rumored that some of the young men used to bind themselves there. All sorts of other ludicrous claims were made. Whispers circulated that Father Josemaría hypnotized people and, using special lighting effects, simulated levitation.

When St. Josemaría first heard about all this, he joked with one of the fellows who went to see him, "Come here and I'll hypnotize you." He also made a joke out of the levitation stories (at the time he was putting on weight, the first sign of severe diabetes):"It would be a first-class miracle if I could levitate even a few inches off the floor."[4]

---

3. Cf. Vázquez de Prada, Vol. II, 315ff.
4. Ibid., 371.

Some people even said the Father was the anti-Christ and the 999 points of his well-known book *The Way* (a classic of Christian spirituality) were an allusion to the number of the beast of the Apocalypse (666), inverted.

It soon became clear that there was more was behind this than just student tales. These silly stories were only the tip of the iceberg. The founder began to hear more serious reports of slander and gossip: Well-known people were beginning to describe his apostolic work as a clandestine heretical sect, a very serious accusation in "officially Catholic" postwar Spain. They said it had Masonic features (the Franco dictatorship had just set up a Tribunal for the Repression of Freemasonry) and in due course would be condemned by the Church and the state.

Some months later, Opus Dei was in fact denounced to the Tribunal for the Repression of Freemasonry as "a branch of Masonry with ties to Jewish sects." Once the judges began to look into the case, they realized how ridiculous the accusation was. After visiting the oratory at Jenner Street, they decided to dismiss the charges.[5]

WHERE WERE THE ATTACKS COMING FROM?

The source

The source of these rumors soon came to light. There was a common denominator among the young men in contact with the Jenner residence in the early months of 1940 who were spreading gossip: all were members of a Marian Congregation for students. The Marian Congregations have done much good over the centuries and in many countries continue doing it now.

---

5. Ibid., 370–371; RHF T-04214.

In those turbulent times, nevertheless, they were the source of the opposition. It was quickly established beyond question that the persecution was begun and fostered by a 35-year-old religious,[6] at the time director of the Spanish Federation of Marian Congregations. He had sent six or seven youth to find out what was going on in the Jenner residence and keep him informed of anything there that "smelled" of heresy.

Father Josemaría's reaction

Father Josemaría suffered greatly because of the campaign. It was especially painful because he had great love for brother priests and for religious, and the person organizing the attack was a priest. Precisely at that time, at the request of the bishops, he was preaching retreats for priests and seminarians in many Spanish dioceses.

He went to see his confessor, Father Valentín Sánchez Ruiz, who advised him to go and talk openly and fraternally with the director of the Congregation, like himself a Jesuit. So Father Josemaría went to see the man and explained in detail what they were doing in the Jenner residence. As a demonstration of good will, he proposed a sort of friendly pact: each would undertake to tell the other in all honesty anything derogatory they heard about Opus Dei or about the Marian Congregation. The director agreed.

On November 14, 1940, Josemaría met him by chance at the entrance to a public building. He records in his *Intimate Notes* that he held out his right hand, without any bitterness, in an unaffected display of charity and friendliness.

---

6. This was Father Angel Carrillo de Albornoz, S.J. In 1940 he was appointed director of the Spanish Federation of Marian Congregations. In 1948 he became Director of the General Secretariat of Marian Congregations. See Vázquez de Prada, Vol. II, 322.

"I'm pleased to see you, Father. God bless you! Don't you remember our gentlemen's agreement?"

But the other priest, claiming to be in a hurry, cut short the conversation and walked away.

The following day Josemaría wrote in his notes:

"Madrid, 15 November. . . . In the afternoon, I found myself experiencing a deep interior joy on account of that tribulation. And I feel sympathy and even affection for the religious causing this whole mess. Besides, I understand that he is a very likable man, and certainly a very good person. May God bless and prosper him!"[7]

Seeking fraternal reconciliation

Although that religious priest, without realizing the extent of his mistake, continued with his campaign, Father Josemaría never stopped trusting in his good will or clarifying the true aims of Opus Dei.

An excerpt from a letter reflects his concern for peaceful reconciliation.

Madrid, May 20, 1941.

My dear brother in the Lord: I write you these lines, filled with cordiality and sincere affection, to make it known to you that one hears on all sides that you are the source of a campaign of defamation against the brother who is writing this letter, and against his poor priestly efforts, which the Holy Church has approved. . . .

I have been told, through various channels, that you intend not to stop until you see Opus Dei destroyed. . . . I am sure

---

7. Ibid., 323; *Intimate Notes*, 1626, November 15, 1940.

that we will end up being good friends. I have nothing toward you except fraternal good will and an earnest desire to forget everything that could obscure that affection.

In the meantime, be assured that we will never utter a word against those who are so cruelly persecuting us. With the grace of God, we will always be prepared to suffer with great joy whatever we may have to suffer for Jesus Christ and for the service of our Mother the Holy Church. That is our vocation.

Your brother and devoted servant in Christ,

J.M. Escrivá, Priest.[8]

The same attitude until he died

From 1947 on, St. Josemaría lived in Rome, where the central offices of Opus Dei are located. Between 1947 and 1950, Opus Dei received all the papal approvals needed as a worldwide institution of pontifical right, with the encouragement and blessing of Pope Pius XII. The old campaigns were over—at least for the time being. One might think he would have felt no obligation to make any new attempt at reconciliation with that religious and would simply have left the past alone.

Nevertheless, they did exchange further letters. In one of them, dated June 3, 1950, when the other man was staying in London (he too had been living in Rome since 1948), Monsignor Escrivá wrote: "When you return to Rome, I hope we can have a long conversation and get together often. . . . With sincere affection, I send my warmest regards and ask your prayers for Opus Dei and for this sinner. *In Domino.*"[9]

---

8. Ibid., 353–354; St. Josemaría's collected letters, EF-410520-1.
9. Ibid., 377; EF-500603-2.

Unfortunately, a short time later, in 1951, a most regrettable thing happened. The religious left the Society of Jesus, quit the priesthood, and abandoned the Catholic faith.

Encarnación Ortega, at the time a director of the apostolic work of the women of Opus Dei, was present when Father Josemaría heard the news. "Monsignor Escrivá was visibly moved and saddened. He buried his head in his hands and fell silent, withdrawing into himself, praying. Then Salvador Canals reminded him that this same man had once organized a very serious campaign of slander against the Work. Monsignor Escrivá interrupted him bluntly, 'But he is a soul, my son, a soul!' "[10] Later on, when he heard that Father Carrillo was seriously ill, he sought to ensure that a priest would go to help him be reconciled with the Church and die in peace with God.

Thus he put into practice what he had always taught: "Don't allow yourself to think badly of anyone, even though the words or actions of the person in question give you reasonable grounds for doing so."[11] St. Josemaría's attitude towards that priest was an echo of Christ's teaching, which he always followed: *Judge not, and you will not be judged; condemn not, and you will not be condemned; forgive, and you will be forgiven.*[12]

IN BARCELONA: "A NEW STORM"

"In 1941," writes St. Josemaría's first biographer, Salvador Bernal, "this opposition became especially acute in Barcelona. Quite a number of young men frequented the Palau center,

---

10. Pilar Urbano, *El hombre de Villa Tevere* (Barcelona: Plaza y Janés, 1995), 120–121; RHF, T-05074, p. 19.

11. *The Way*, 442.

12. Lk 6:37.

a little apartment in Balmes Street, near Aragon Street. It was rented by Alfonso Balcells who, though he hadn't asked to join Opus Dei, offered to help because he was the only one who had finished his degree. Although in those days probably no more than half a dozen people in Barcelona had requested to join, all of them still students, a big ruckus was raised against the Work."[13]

Initially there was much similarity between the events in Barcelona and in Madrid. For example, like the Jenner residence and all the centers of Opus Dei, the little apartment on Balmes Street had a plain black wooden cross. The bishop of Madrid, and later Pope Pius XII as well, granted indulgences to the faithful who devoutly kissed the cross in centers of Opus Dei or prayed before it. As the founder wrote in no. 178 of *The Way*: "Whenever you see a poor, wooden cross, alone, uncared-for, worthless . . . and without a corpus, don't forget that that cross is *your* cross: the everyday hidden cross, unattractive and unconsoling—the cross that is waiting for the corpus it lacks: and that corpus must be you." Ordinary life, with its sacrifices and daily work, hidden, unspectacular, unrewarding, can be a great occasion for holiness, when it is embraced out of love for God and one's neighbor.

As in Madrid, the story also got around that students took turns crucifying themselves on this cross in some sort of bloody ritual. To prevent the harm this slander could do, Father Josemaría had to replace the cross with a much smaller one. "This way they won't be able to say we are crucifying ourselves, because there just isn't room," he explained.[14]

---

13. Bernal, 265.
14. Alfonso Balcells: *Memoria Ingenua* (Madrid: Rialp, 2009), 155.

Similar mistaken ideas

Deceived by the stories about Opus Dei, some priests and religious worried that if the idea got abroad that the laity could become saints in the world through work and the fulfillment of their daily duties, religious orders whose members live apart from the world in monasteries and convents would end up losing vocations.[15]

Some people even thought that St. Josemaría's teaching on the "universal call to holiness," which the Second Vatican Council later declared a fundamental part of Catholic doctrine,[16] would cause vocations to the religious state to drop off and was even heretical. The conventional wisdom of the time was that to seek holiness it was necessary to renounce the world and enter a seminary, monastery, or house of formation.

The point is illustrated by something that happened to the mother of Amadeo de Fuenmayor, a law student from Valencia and a member of the Work, who later became a professor of civil law and eventually a priest, a canon lawyer, and professor of ecclesiastical law.

Amadeo describes how on a certain occasion his mother went to Barcelona to see one of her daughters there. "She was visited by a priest she had never met in her life, who asked her if she was my mother, and told her that her son was 'in danger of being condemned.'" She had to persuade him to abandon the path he was taking, the priest said. One of the principal reasons was that "members of Opus Dei have been deceived into believing that it is possible to be holy in the midst of the world."[17]

---

15. Vázquez de Prada, Vol. II, 390–391.

16. Vatican II, Dogmatic Constitution *Lumen Gentium*, ch. 6.

17. Vázquez de Prada, Vol. II, 369.

SOME EVENTS AND THEIR REPERCUSSIONS

First, expulsions

Alfonso Balcells, at the time a recently qualified doctor—later, professor of clinical pathology and President of the University of Salamanca—was a member of the Marian Congregation of Barcelona. In his book *Memoria ingenua* he tells what happened one Sunday at the weekly meeting of the congregation:

"One Sunday, when I was at the weekly meeting of the sodality, the Father Director, Father Vergés, called me aside and without any preliminaries told me that I was 'expelled from the sodality.' Obviously I was surprised and had no idea what his reason was. When I asked him, 'But Father, why?' he just pointed to the door and said, 'You are expelled as a traitor and a Judas to the sodality.'"[18]

Balcells recounts that the priest then proceeded to expel other members of the sodality who frequented Palau, the small Opus Dei center. He thought it was his moral duty to do so (he was known to be decisive and autocratic, but a good and honest man). Acting on information from Madrid, Vergés had from the start a distorted image of Opus Dei, and took it for granted that it was a "danger" to the Church and the Marian Congregations. As in Madrid, he acted on the basis of complaints by some young men who at his request had stationed themselves in a coffee shop in Balmes Street, just across the road from Palau.

The irony is that Alfonso Balcells, though so dramatically expelled, was not a member of Opus Dei and only went to the Work's apartment very infrequently. He came to their attention

---

18. Balcells, 138.

because, being the only university graduate there, he allowed his name to be used to sign the lease for the apartment.

Years later, Balcells wrote: "What happened simply was that Father Vergés had a bad day. It could happen to anybody. He acted with the best of intentions, based on information from people whom up to then he had trusted completely. The fact is that later on he recognized his mistake; that is what's important."[19]

Card-carrying heretics

The six or seven young men who continued going to Palau didn't find it easy to keep calm and forgive repeatedly. They were living in a climate of moral terrorism, suffering what Balcells calls a "moral lynching,"[20] regarded with horror and the objects of insults in many Catholic circles. Worst of all, there were painful misunderstandings within their own families.

One of their number, Laureano López Rodó, recalls how Father Pascual Galindo, a friend of Father Josemaría, arranged for all the young men connected with the Work to attend Mass the next day in a school run by nuns. "The superior and another nun present there were very 'edified,' and they invited us to have breakfast with Father Galindo. In the middle of breakfast, Father Pascual said to the superior, 'These are the heretics for whose conversion you asked me to offer the Mass.' The poor nun almost fainted. She'd been made to believe that we were a vast legion of card-carrying heretics, and she found that we were a handful of ordinary, run-of-the-mill students who attended Mass devoutly and received Communion."[21]

---

19. Ibid., 144.
20. See ibid., 162.
21. Vázquez de Prada, Vol. II, 350, note 76; RHF, T-04606.

The uproar reaches the governor

Things got worse when the director of the sodality, who was highly regarded in Barcelona, lodged a complaint against the Work and its founder with the city's civil governor. At the beginning of the dictatorship, the borderline between religion and politics was impossible to make out. Any group denounced as a heretical or Masonic sect and condemned by high-ranking clerics was regarded by the new social order as a threat to national security. So the governor, Antonio Correa Veglison, instructed the police that if the Reverend Escrivá set foot in Barcelona, he should be arrested at once.

The papal nuncio to Spain, Archbishop Cicognani, knowing that Opus Dei had the approval and support of ecclesiastical authority, became aware of this, and advised Father Josemaría to travel to Barcelona under a false name.[22]

Shortly afterward, the governor decided that the matter required urgent handling. One day in the middle of May 1941 he sent an order to Palau for the legal representative of the organization or, failing that, the holder of the lease on the apartment, to answer the charges.[23]

Balcells, who had rented the apartment, was the one who had to go. The governor opened the conversation by saying: "I know everything, and all you people are going to end up in jail. Don't you know it's an occult sect?" Then he launched into a long, tedious harangue.

Balcells remained unruffled and, after insisting on being listened to respectfully, managed to calm down the governor a bit and explain Opus Dei, Palau, and what went on there. After many questions, Correa finally limited himself to telling Balcells

22. See Balcells, 159.
23. See ibid., 122.

57

to be very careful. Years later, Balcells provided medical care to the governor—by then a good friend.

After the storm in Barcelona had died down, the first Opus Dei student residence (the Colegio Mayor Monterols, at no. 3 Atenas Street) came to be built, St. Josemaría had words of Christ from St. John's Gospel inscribed in large letters in the oratory: *Veritas liberabit vos.* "The truth will set you free."[24]

PRAY, BE SILENT, FORGIVE, WORK, AND SMILE

Although less intense, storms resembling the one in Barcelona also broke out in Valencia, Saragossa, Bilbao, and in general wherever Opus Dei was starting its apostolic work.[25]

Rafael Termes, a 22-year old engineering student who was the director of Palau, wrote of St. Josemaría's attitude at the time: "He showed great supernatural understanding and charity toward those who were attacking him, and always tried to excuse them, saying they did it *putantes se obsequium praestare Deo* (thinking they were offering service to God, Jn 16:2), and exhorted us to love them, as he did, seeing them as God's instrument to help the Work mature." The Father was very happy to have Rafael's assurance in a letter that he shouldn't worry because none of them had let slip a single uncharitable word.

Salvador Bernal says that Father Josemaría "taught them, with his example and word, to forgive those unseeing detractors at once and without hesitation. When anyone brought news to him of a new falsehood, which often happened several times a

---

24. Jn 8:32.
25. See Vázquez de Prada, Vol. II, 350.

day, his first reaction was to invite them to say an Our Father or a Hail Mary for the person who had slandered them."[26]

"Mercedes Morado and Begoña Alvarez, who in Rome assisted Monsignor Escrivá over a number of years with their work, wrote that his spirit of forgiveness and understanding toward those who slandered him was something that grew progressively, to the point that he could say in all simplicity, 'I don't feel any resentment toward them. I pray for them every day, just as hard as I pray for my children. And by praying for them so much, I've come to love them with the same heart and the same intensity that I love my children.' "[27]

Bernal recounts that besides praying daily at Holy Mass for his sons and daughters in Opus Dei and his own parents, St. Josemaría prayed "for those who are still living and want to trouble us, and for those who have slandered us and have already gone to render an account with our Lord. I say: 'Lord, I forgive them so that you may forgive them and so that you may forgive our sins.' "[28]

From the first attacks, the response urged by the Father, and which his children tried to follow, was clear and positive: "silence, work, forgiveness; smile, pray, and suffer joyfully . . . place yourselves in our Lord's hands and don't forget that He doesn't lose battles."[29] "What difficult times those were!" said Father Alvaro del Portillo, St. Josemaría's first successor, many years later, "and how alone the Father was . . . How silent he remained! I recall now the letter he wrote us in which he prohibited us from talking about what was going on, even among ourselves."[30]

---

26. See Bernal, 259–273.

27. Urbano, 120; AGP, RHF, T-07902, T-04861.

28. Bernal, 272.

29. Vázquez de Prada, Vol. II, 387–388.

30. Notes from his preaching, December 25, 1976.

A platinum scalpel

The bishop of Madrid, Leopoldo Eijo y Garay, knew Josemaría very well and had a high regard for him. He had followed the birth and development of Opus Dei with interest and affection. He was also aware of the attacks and slanders and did what he could to stop them. He greatly admired the spirit of pardon and forgiveness of Monsignor Escrivá and his sons, and expressed that admiration both orally and in writing, but he had one small doubt: with the passing of time, would future members of Opus Dei who learned of what had happened have the same forgiving attitude? He said as much to Alvaro del Portillo on the day in 1943 when he ordained him to the priesthood.

"Don't worry," replied Father Alvaro. "We realize that God allows this so that the sacrifice he sends us will make us better, and that we should be happy, because when a good surgeon wants to carry out an operation properly he chooses a good instrument; and God has chosen a platinum scalpel for these difficulties."

The bishop mentioned later how impressed he had been by this, especially when Alvaro told him that he had often heard the founder use the scalpel metaphor. "Like father, like son!" said Bishop Leopoldo.[31]

On May 2, 1941 St. Josemaría wrote to Rafael Termes, director of Palau, commenting on some words in St. Paul's letter to the Romans (Rom 12:12):

"My dear sons: We should rejoice that our Lord has seen fit to treat us in a divine manner. What can I tell you? Be happy, *spe gaudentes*, rejoicing in hope. Bear suffering with charity, with never a word against anyone; *in tribulatione patientes!*, patient in tribulation. And be filled with a spirit of prayer, *orationi instantes!*, constant in prayer.

---

31. See de Acevedo, *Missão Cumprida*, 78–79.

"My sons: the dawn can already be discerned, and what a great harvest there will be, in that blessed Barcelona, when the new day comes!"[32]

CONSOLATION IN TRIBULATION

The parents of some of the young men of the Work in Barcelona, distressed by the accusations against Escrivá and Opus Dei and at the same time disconcerted by their sons' resolute determination in their vocation, decided to consult the most highly regarded Catholic personage in Catalonia.[33] This was the abbot of the Benedictine monastery of Montserrat, guardian of the sanctuary of the patroness of Catalonia. Montserrat has always been the principal source of Christian faith and culture in Catalonia. In the 1940s the abbot coadjutor was Dom Aureli María Escarré, O.S.B., a man of great distinction.

Dom Aureli prudently avoided being drawn into the heated arguments. Learning that Escrivá's superior was the bishop of Madrid, he wrote the bishop on May 9, 1941, asking for clarification.

Bishop Leopoldo hastened to reply. The full text of this letter and of a second, longer one systematically rebutting the slanders against Escrivá and Opus Dei can be found in one of the appendices of volume II of Vázquez de Prada's biography.

"Father Escrivá," said the bishop in his first letter, "is an exemplary priest, chosen by God for the sanctification of many souls. . . . In a word, I have nothing to say against that Opus. It is, I repeat, truly Dei [of God]. . . . I am aware of all the accusations which have been made; I know they are all false."

---

32. Vázquez de Prada, Vol. II, 346.

33. Ibid., 348ff. and Appendices IV and V.

In the second letter, dated June 21, he stated emphatically: "What is really amazing is the spirit with which the members of Opus Dei have borne this great trial. . . . I admire and am edified by the holy joy with which they suffer for their vocation, which the gale only serves to embed more deeply in their souls. There is not one complaint or word of ill will toward the religious who so harshly persecute them. Their greatest consolation is seeing that all the bishops in whose territories they have houses are with them; that we are encouraging and defending them."

Thanks to the information from the bishop, the abbot was extremely helpful in reassuring the families in Barcelona, and became a good friend of St. Josemaría. They saw each other frequently in the following years.[34]

Drowning evil in an abundance of good

Rev. Dr José López Ortiz, professor of the history of law at the University of Madrid and later bishop of Tuy (Santiago de Compostela), was a close friend of Farther Josemaría. Renowned for his intellect and learning, he helped to clear up the confusion among well-intentioned people.

"I could see that Josemaría Escrivá's response to those attacks—some of them quite horrific—was always very supernatural and charitable. But I would emphasize that this was not an unfeeling, stoic reaction, but rather one replete with prayer and mortification, and with total confidence in God.

"Whenever we spoke, he used to say that if God allowed this to happen, it was for the good, and that of course he forgave everyone involved. At the same time, he expressed a serene and just indignation because of the love he had for his sons, whom

---

34. See Balcells, 164.

he saw being unjustly persecuted, and because of the harm this in turn was doing to the Church and to souls."[35]

When the persecution extended to others besides himself and engulfed innocent people, whether members of Opus Dei or not, St. Josemaría fought hard for truth and justice. First, as we've seen, he sought dialogue and reconciliation with the responsible parties. At the same time, he kept the Church authorities informed—the bishops, and the Holy See from 1946 onward—not to have the culprits punished, but so that the bishops and the pope would know the full truth about Opus Dei and its members' activities, and could in turn communicate the truth about Opus Dei factually, authoritatively, and credibly. That happened both with the pope (Pius XII approved Opus Dei as a worldwide institution of pontifical right, provisionally in 1947 and definitively in 1950), and with most of the bishops of Spain.

Here was his plan of battle: forgive and excuse, fight untiringly "to drown evil in an abundance of good," and combat lies with truth.

THE SHOCK WAVE REACHES ROME

In 1947 Father Escrivá, and a handful of members of Opus Dei began the apostolate of the Work in the Eternal City. Soon young men became acquainted with fellow students who became interested in the message of holiness and apostolate in the world that St. Josemaría presented so attractively. And just as happened elsewhere, some of these felt God's call to this way of life and asked to join Opus Dei.

The first Roman vocations had hardly emerged when the same charges leveled at Father Josemaría and his work in Spain

---

35. de Acevedo, *Uma Luz no Mundo*, 166; AGP, RHF 4214.

appeared in Rome. What happened there was a carbon copy of what had happened in Madrid and Barcelona—religious, probably badly informed by colleagues in Spain, began to spread the same stories among the families of the first Italian members of Opus Dei. They went to see the families, warned them, frightened them, and created a painful climate of suspicion and tension in the families.[36]

A complaint to the Pope

A student named Umberto Farri met St. Josemaría in 1949 and asked to join Opus Dei. Later for many years he would work in cooperation with the Italian government and the European Union on an aid program to educate poor people in Third World countries. But in 1949 he was only a student, and his story is typical of what happened in this persecution. It's easier to understand if we begin at the end.

Umberto's father, Francesco, died at a ripe old age in 1985. Going through his papers, his son to his surprise came across a carefully concealed "private archive" documenting the history of that Roman persecution. There he found a photocopy of a letter of complaint against St. Josemaría and Opus Dei addressed to the pope and signed first by Francesco Farri and then also by the fathers of four other young Italian members of Opus Dei (one of whom withdrew his name before the letter was sent). It was dated April 25, 1951, almost a year after Pius XII had approved Opus Dei definitively.

Along with the photocopy of the letter to the pope, the archive also contained earlier drafts, with changes and suggestions added by hand by a certain religious. There were also thirteen letters from the same individual to Francesco,

---

encouraging him to make the complaint to the pope in the form of a petition from a group of parents, and advising him on how to proceed.

Umberto learned about this only thirty-four years after the event. Neither his father nor St. Josemaría had ever uttered a single word to him about it.[37]

Untiring in forgiveness

Umberto knew nothing at the time, but St. Josemaría knew everything about what was going on. As during the hostility in Spain in 1941, he asked his sons to be silent, to pray, to smile, and to work. And also to love their parents more and to be even more considerate of them.

They all did what he advised: none spoke about those unpleasant events. One of these young men was Mario Lantini, who later became Regional Vicar of Opus Dei in Italy. He never mentioned his problems with his family until thirty-two years later, in 1983, when giving evidence at Josemaría's process of beatification. "He was reluctant," he said then, "to go into what happened 'because Monsignor Escrivá always forbade us, explicitly, to speak of this, lest we fail in charity, even when talking among ourselves; as it says in a point of *The Way*: When you can't praise, say nothing.' No one in Opus Dei knew what had happened except those involved, the founder, and Father Alvaro, at that time Counselor of the Italian region." Father Alvaro, in turn, said he never heard the Father utter "one single word of recrimination against those who defamed him, even in the most trying moments."[38]

---

37. See ibid., Vol. III, 191–192.
38. Ibid., 139

Two incidents of note

The story doesn't end there. And upon discovering its ending, Umberto was deeply touched. Some years after the complaint, his father asked to see St. Josemaría. When they met, he fell on his knees in front of St. Josemaría, tearfully asking forgiveness. The Father embraced him warmly, and said he had understood and had forgiven him right from the start; he was certain that he had acted properly, because he did so in good faith, believing on the basis of a deception that he was acting in his son's best interests.

Apart from staying silent and forgiving, St. Josemaría's response to the opposition in Rome was to pray even more intensely. On May 14, 1951, he gathered some of his sons together in an oratory still under construction in Villa Tevere (the central offices of Opus Dei in Rome) and held a simple ceremony, in which he consecrated the families of the members of Opus Dei to the Holy Family. He beseeched God, among other things, to "instill in their hearts an ever-growing appreciation of the beauty of our vocation . . . make them always share in the joy and peace that you grant us as a reward for our dedication."[39] Since then, this consecration has been renewed yearly in all the centers of Opus Dei on the feast of the Holy Family.

WHERE FREEDOM IS NOT LOVED

Moving on from the "friendly fire" coming from religious circles, we turn now to slanders propagated by the standard-bearers of Franco's dictatorship.

In those tumultuous years of the 1940s, Father José López Ortiz, mentioned above, was sent a "confidential report on the

---

39. Ibid., 141.

secret organization Opus Dei," prepared by the intelligence service of the Falange, the only political party allowed under the dictatorship. The document originated in Madrid and was dated January 16, 1942.

Father López Ortiz, a good friend of Josemaría Escrivá, grew very indignant on reading the report. "On one occasion," he later recalled, "I was shown an internal document of the Falange in which he was grossly slandered. I considered it my duty to show him this document which a friend had lent me. The attacks were so savage that I could not keep myself from crying as he calmly read those sheets. He finished reading and, seeing me so upset, he burst out laughing, saying: 'Don't worry Pepe, because everything they say here is false, thank God. But if they knew me better, they could have said far worse things because I am nothing but a wretched sinner who is madly in love with Jesus Christ.' Instead of tearing up that string of insults he gave the papers back to me so that my friend could return them to party headquarters, which was where he had taken them from. 'Take them,' he said, 'and give them to your friend so that he can put them back and that way they won't start persecuting him.' "[40]

Among other things, the document accused him of having an "internationalist" outlook, of being opposed to the mindset of Franco's government, of criticizing the system of appointing professors, the awarding of scholarships, etc. Even more—hard to believe, for someone unfamiliar with the Falange's techniques—it stated falsely that the Jenner residence contained a map of Germany covered with pigs representing not pig production but the German people.

St. Josemaría was quick to uphold the truth: "Opus Dei, which is free from any concern regarding earthly ambitions,

---

40. Ibid., Vol. II, 372.

seeks only 'the Christian perfection of its members through the sanctification of ordinary work' . . . God has permitted us to suffer, as the main opposition, persecution by good people. And joining those good people are others who are not so good, who hate the Holy Church and Catholic Spain.' "[41] "Others call such people their enemies," he said elsewhere, "You should call them 'benefactors.' Pray to God for them: as a result, you will come to like them."[42]

Unscrupulous politicians took advantage of the hostile atmosphere created by the "good" to add fuel to the flames. Those flames have continued to spread over the years, continually fed with more fuel, and have not yet been extinguished. Nor are they likely ever to be, for the Church is destined to be persecuted until the end of the world.

St. Josemaría wrote: "The worst thing is, certainly, that these misrepresentations and false interpretations . . . will remain embedded in many people's minds . . . and become the cause of an incredible obstinacy to recognizing the truth."[43]

The minister gets involved

In the 1960s, nearly twenty years after these events and still during the Franco regime, some members of Opus Dei, making use of their right to express their opinion freely, published articles in which they proposed a greater pluralism in the trade union movement. At that time, Spain had only a single trade union and a single political party, both run by the Falange.

Vázquez de Prada relates: "This sparked violent outbursts in the regime's newspaper chain (the Movement Press) and in

---

41. From a letter to Father Fermín Y. Lorca, EF-420108.

42. St. Josemaría Escrivá, *The Forge*, no. 802.

43. Vázquez de Prada, Vol. II, 387.

Pueblo, a daily paper put out by the Spanish Labor Organization. Monsignor Escrivá had to intervene." He did so for two reasons of justice: to defend innocent people from slander involving the distortion of facts and above all to offer an energetic defense of the inalienable right of his children to act with complete Christian freedom in temporal matters, whether political, cultural, or social.

After Florencio Sánchez Bella, the Counselor of Opus Dei in Spain, tried without results to have the matter clarified, St. Josemaría wrote a letter—clear and blunt, but very charitable—to José Solís Ruiz, secretary general of the Movement (a cabinet position). Among other things, referring to the campaign he said:

"I'm sure that by now you must be aware of the gross mistake being made, and of the responsibility in conscience which all those involved in this campaign are assuming before God's tribunal. For it is a great mistake to denigrate an institution which does not—and cannot—influence the use that its members, spread over five continents, make of their personal freedom as citizens, while never evading their personal responsibility for their actions. I beg you to put an end to this campaign against Opus Dei, since Opus Dei has done nothing to deserve it. . . . Fight when you must (though I am not fond of fighting). But don't commit the injustice of dragging into those battles what lies above all human passions."[44]

In her biography, journalist Pilar Urbano recounts an incident relating to this matter. One day in January, 1967, speaking in Rome with César Ortiz-Echagüe, an architect and member of Opus Dei who had recently arrived from Spain, Monsignor Escrivá told him he was very unhappy with the lack of political

---

44. EF 661028-1.

freedom in Spain. He added: "I have written a strong letter to Minister Solís. I don't expect him to answer, but if he does, I have a few more things I'd like to add! And you for your part can't allow newspapers run by the state, mouthpieces of the government you all pay for, to insult the Work gratuitously."

Urbano goes on to say that when it was a matter of personal attacks or insults, St. Josemaría always recommended an attitude of forgiveness. In this context, she quotes the words of one of the first members of Opus Dei, Rafael Calvo Serer, a professor and Monarchist politician, who had to leave Spain after public demonstrations against the Franco regime. "In 1962, I went to see him in Rome. I unburdened my heart and told him about the calumnies and persecutions I was being subjected to by certain petty officials of the Franco regime. Monsignor Escrivá listened and then said: 'My son, it is hard, but you have to learn how to forgive.' He was silent for a moment and then, as if thinking out loud, he added: 'I didn't need to learn how to forgive, because God has taught me how to love.' "[45]

A permanent lesson

This same spirit of forgiveness was displayed in Argentina in a warm get-together with thousands of people in 1974, when the country was suffering from political upheavals and violence. One of the participants asked the Father why in his ten years of contact with Opus Dei no one had spoken to him about politics and he had not encountered any promotional material relating to political parties. St. Josemaría answered: "But I have been in Opus Dei for 47 years and I have never spoken about politics. I would rather cut out my tongue."

---

45. Urbano, 121; AGP-RHF 21165, p. 294.

He was speaking, naturally, from his position as a priest. Earlier, in the same setting, he had explained that the priest's mission requires that he not get involved in party politics because he has to be a "father" to all. "He should stick to his spiritual mission—which is no small thing!—with his arms wide open to welcome everyone: those on the right and those on the left, those in front, those behind, everybody, everybody, everybody! We can't refuse our hand to anyone! We can't be partisan! We can't speak about strife! We need to talk about understanding, about exchanging points of view in order to reach agreement. But strife, hatred: never!"

Replying to the questioner, a married professional man, he added: "But you can speak about politics with your friends, like any other citizen. But me, No! My advice is that you respect one another, that you get along with one another, walk together in peace, that you don't wish anyone evil. Otherwise, you won't be the friends of freedom that you say you are! We want each citizen to act freely, all of them. And then, that they understand one another, that they don't mistreat one another, not even verbally. Therefore, if you ever hear that I have been slandered, I forgive them from the very start, and besides I love them very much. Tell them that. It hurts me a lot that they lie, but I won't call them liars; their conscience will be the one to do so: liars and scandalmongers!"[46]

Many other such stories could be told. Now, though, we turn to another moral quality very much present in St. Josemaría's life, his ability to apologize. As readily as he forgave others, he would ask for forgiveness when he thought he had hurt someone or treated him unjustly.

---

46. Notes from a get-together of catechesis, Buenos Aires, June 18, 1974.

A MAN WHO KNEW HOW TO APOLOGIZE

Only a person who can ask for forgiveness is genuine when forgiving. This was a characteristic of St. Josemaría throughout his life, and not only in dramatic moments.

He often spoke about the "joy of rectifying." "Precisely because he was so straightforward," explains Bishop Javier Echevarría, "he never had any difficulty rectifying whenever he had been mistaken or when he received new information about a situation. If necessary, he apologized and would say, 'I am not a river that can't flow backwards.' "[47]

He was not afraid of losing face with others nor did he think saying he was sorry would undermine his authority. "I assure you," he used to say, "that correcting yourself rids your soul of bitterness."[48] In fact, asking forgiveness made him very happy. One day in Opus Dei's central offices in Rome, he forcefully scolded two or three people in the main office for some important mistakes in a document they were preparing that they'd overlooked and that could confuse readers. "After a while he came back," writes Pilar Urbano, "looking peaceful and happy. 'My sons, I've just been to confession to Don Alvaro, because what I said to you before was something I had to say, but I shouldn't have said it the way I did. So I asked our Lord to forgive me, and now I've come to ask you to forgive me.' "[49]

Stories about his willingness to rectify could fill a book. These everyday incidents, even more than extraordinary events, are the true measure of greatness.

---

47. Echevarría, 137.
48. Urbano, 350.
49. Ibid., 353.

Sorry for not having listened to an explanation

Alvaro del Portillo witnessed a small instance.

I remember, one day in January 1955, I was on my way home around noon, and I was passing in front of the oratory of St. Gabriel, at our headquarters. There I happened to meet our Father; he was with some students of the Roman College of the Holy Cross, among whom was Fernando Acaso.[50] After greeting the Father, I took the opportunity to tell Fernando that he could now go and get certain pieces of furniture which we needed, because we finally had enough money in the bank.

Well, as soon as he heard that, our founder begged pardon of that son of his. What had happened was this. Just a little before my arrival, the Father had asked about those pieces of furniture. Fernando started to explain why he had not gone to pick them up, but our Father, without letting him continue, asked him again if he had picked them up. Then Fernando simply said no, and our founder said that he did not like us making excuses. But now, having heard what I said, he realized immediately what had happened, and he hastened to apologize, right there in front of us, for not having let Fernando explain.

And as if that were not enough, later on, in the sitting room, in the presence of all the students of the Roman College, he once again asked Fernando's pardon and praised his humility. The quickness with which he made amends was truly remarkable, and he did not hesitate to do so in public if he felt that was called for.[51]

---

50. Later ordained priest, he was involved in starting the apostolate of Opus Dei in Japan.

51. Alvaro del Portillo, *Immersed in God* (New York: Scepter Publishers, 1996), 82–83.

A hasty reply

On another occasion, while walking hurriedly along a passage-way in Villa Tevere, he met a daughter of his who tried to detain him to ask him something not very important or urgent. Almost without breaking his stride, St. Josemaría said to her, "How should I know? Ask Don Alvaro!"

Later that day, the same girl was tidying up some things in the hall of Villa Vecchia, as Monsignor Escrivá and Don Alvaro went by. They stopped for a moment, and Monsignor Escrivá said, "I'm sorry, my daughter, for having answered you as I did earlier. Those of you who live with me have so much to put up with!"[52]

A piece of torn paper

The protagonist of this next story was Bishop Javier Echevarría, at the time a young priest and Monsignor Escrivá's secretary, now Prelate of Opus Dei and his second successor. In 1968 St. Josemaría and a few others from Villa Tevere were spending part of the summer in a village in the north of Italy. The Father took the opportunity to work on a document for his children's formation.

A few days before leaving, he made a big push to finish revising what he was working on. He gave Father Javier Echevarría some pages to put in order, and a short time later Father Javier returned to the room where Escrivá was working. "Father, there's a page missing. It must be somewhere here."

"No, it isn't. It's not here. Look for it, because I've given them all to you."

Father Javier went over the pages again and made certain that one was missing. "Father, I've searched for it carefully and that page is definitely missing."

---

52. Urbano, 353.

Monsignor Escrivá answered him impatiently, "Well, it isn't here. You must have dropped it somewhere."

Father Javier looked at the wastepaper basket beside the desk, which was full to the brim. "Maybe it's in that basket," he said. "You may have torn it up by mistake."

The Father continued writing and didn't answer. Father Javier picked up the basket and took it into the room he was using as his office. In less than three minutes, Monsignor Escrivá quietly came in and found Father Javier engrossed in the intricate task of assembling a jigsaw-puzzle of bits of paper, which little by little revealed the lost page of the document.

"Javi, my son, I'm sorry!" exclaimed Monsignor Escrivá. "You were right. And to crown it all, look at all the extra work I'm giving you. I'm the one who should have searched more thoroughly; you've taught me a lesson so that next time I won't be so sure of myself."

And he stayed there, helping Father Javier almost timidly by cutting pieces of adhesive tape to stick the pieces of paper together. He kept begging his pardon, with sincere sorrow. "And besides forgiving me," he said, "I want you to offer up the bother I've caused you for me. You can see how much I need you to help me to work better and improve!"[53]

"I beg your forgiveness"

He was also quick to heal any wound he might have inadvertently caused. "On another occasion in Rome," writes Pilar Urbano, "he reprimanded Ernesto Julia on the intercom for not doing an important job. Ernesto did not protest or make any excuse.

---

53. Ibid., 405–406.

Shortly afterward, someone informed Monsignor Escrivá that Ernesto had not known about the matter because he had not been asked to do it. Immediately, without delaying a second, Monsignor Escrivá picked up the intercom again and asked Ernesto to come see him. When Ernesto arrived, he found Monsignor Escrivá waiting for him with his arms wide open to welcome him. With a warm, affectionate smile he said, "My son, I'm sorry. I beg your forgiveness and restore your good name to you!"[54]

The frustrated journalist

Barajas Airport, Madrid 1970. Monsignor Escrivá was making a stop-over on his way from Rome to Mexico. Photographers came to the international departure area, hoping to get shots of the founder of Opus Dei. Eduardo Caliz, a heavy-set man who was a photographer for the *Nuevo Diario*, opened up a path through the crowd surrounding Monsignor Escrivá and said, "Let's have a few photos!"

"Look," replied Monsignor Escrivá, "I'm not Concha Piquer [a famous singer]. I'm only a poor man!"

"This isn't for me, but I have to do my job. It's how I feed my children," the photographer replied.

Monsignor Escrivá stopped short. Looking Eduardo in the eye, he smiled as if he had found a long-lost friend.

"If you have to do your job, and earn your children's bread and butter, I'll stay here and pose until you tell me to stop!"[55]

In these pages we have seen examples of something St. Paul earnestly recommended to the early Christians: *Be kind to one*

---

54. See ibid., 351.
55. Ibid., 354–355.

another, tender-hearted, forgiving one another, as God in Christ forgave you.[56] *Do not be overcome by evil, but overcome evil with good.*[57]

We have seen St. Josemaría's capacity to forgive in extremely difficult circumstances during the 1930s and 1940s, a time of persecution, war, fierce hatred, misunderstanding, calumnies by the "good," and the devious ways of the dictatorship. We ended on a more peaceful note, looking at forgiveness in everyday life.

At all times—dramatic and prosaic—there were reflected in Josemaría Escrivá the Christian virtues of humility, love for God, and love for neighbor. These are features that trace the profile of a saint "who knew how to forgive."

---

56. Eph 4:32.
57. Rom 12:21.

APPENDIX I

ON THE LIFE AND MESSAGE OF
ST. JOSEMARÍA ESCRIVÁ

I. BIOGRAPHY

St. Josemaría Escrivá de Balaguer was born in Barbastro, in northern Spain, on January 9, 1902. He started his ecclesiastical studies in the Seminary of Logroño in 1918, and in 1920 continued at the Seminary of St. Francis de Paula in Saragossa, where in 1922 he became a superior or prefect. In 1923 he began to study civil law at the University of Saragossa. He was ordained to the priesthood on March 28, 1925.

He began his work as a priest in rural parishes, then carried on pastoral work in the poor districts and hospitals of Madrid, and among university students.

On October 2, 1928, by divine inspiration he founded Opus Dei, which has opened up in the Church a new path among people of all social classes for seeking holiness and carrying out apostolate, through the sanctification of ordinary work and the tasks of each day.

Opus Dei from the beginning received approval from the diocesan ecclesiastical authority and was approved by the Holy See in 1943. On November 28, 1982, Pope John Paul II erected it as a personal prelature.

Monsignor Escrivá obtained a doctorate in law from the University of Madrid and a doctorate in theology from the Lateran University in Rome. He was awarded an honorary doctorate by the University of Saragossa. He was Chancellor of the University of Navarra (Pamplona, Spain) and of the University of Piura (Peru). Earlier he had been a lecturer in ethics and professional morality at the School of Journalism in Madrid and lecturer in canon law and Roman law in Saragossa and Madrid.

He was a consulter to the Pontifical Commission for the authentic interpretation of the Code of Canon Law and to the Sacred Congregation for Seminaries and Universities. He was a Domestic Prelate and an honorary Academician of the Pontifical Roman Academy of Theology.

In 1946 he took up residence in Rome, setting up the central offices of Opus Dei in the Eternal City. He died there on June 26, 1975, with a reputation for holiness. His mortal remains rest in the prelatic Church of Our Lady of Peace.

Among his published writings, apart from the theological and legal study *La Abadesa de la Huelgas*, are books of spirituality that have been translated into numerous languages: *The Way*, *Holy Rosary*, *Christ Is Passing By*, *Friends of God*, *The Way of the Cross*, *In Love with the Church*, *Furrow*, and *The Forge* (the last five titles were published posthumously). Another book, containing press interviews, has the title *Conversations with Monsignor Escrivá*.

Monsignor Escrivá was canonized by Pope John Paul II in St. Peter's Square on October 6, 2002. St. Josemaría's feast day is celebrated on June 26.

II. ST. JOSEMARÍA ESCRIVÁ'S MESSAGE

The universal call to holiness: holiness in the middle of the world

Following a Mass of Thanksgiving on October 7, 2002, the day after St. Josemaría's canonization, Pope John Paul II addressed the pilgrims. He told them: "Saint Josemaría was chosen by the Lord to proclaim the universal call to holiness and to indicate that everyday life, its customary activities, are a path towards holiness. It could be said that he was the *saint of the ordinary*. He was really convinced that, for whoever lives with an outlook of faith, everything offers an opportunity for a meeting with God, everything becomes a stimulus for prayer. Seen in that way, daily life reveals an unsuspected greatness. Holiness is really put on everyone's doorstep."

In 1968 St. Josemaría was interviewed by two journalists from *L'Osservatore della Domenica*. They asked, "What is the role Opus Dei has fulfilled, and is at present fulfilling?" His response was: "The purpose of Opus Dei is to foster the search for holiness and the carrying out of the apostolate by Christians who live in the world, whatever their state in life or position in society.

"The Work was born to help those Christians, who through their family, their friendships, their ordinary work, their aspirations, form part of the very texture of civil society, to understand that their life, just as it is, can be an opportunity for meeting Christ: that it is a way of holiness and apostolate. Christ is present in any honest human activity. The life of an ordinary Christian, which to some people may seem banal and petty, can and should be a holy and sanctifying life."[1]

In other words, to follow Christ, to be of service to the Church, to help others to recognize their destiny on earth, "there

---

1. *Conversations with Monsignor Escrivá*, no. 60.

is no need to leave the world or keep it at arm's length. . . . you don't even need to take up an ecclesiastical activity."[2]

In *The Way*, St. Josemaría wrote: "You have an obligation to sanctify yourself. Yes, you too. Who thinks that this task is only for priests and religious? To everyone, without exception, our Lord said: *Be perfect, as my Heavenly Father is perfect.*"[3]

Years later, in the sixth chapter of *Lumen Gentium*, the central document of the Second Vatican Council, the Church stressed this teaching, rooted in the Gospel, by proclaiming the *universal call to holiness* of all the baptized, underlining the importance of the baptismal vocation.

Divine filiation as the foundation

The significance of the baptismal vocation common to all Christians was a theme St. Josemaría developed in great depth. All the baptized, incorporated into Christ through the sacrament of Baptism, receive *the power to become children of God* (*Jn* 1:12) through the grace of the Holy Spirit. They consequently receive the power to live every moment and every circumstance of life with a spirit of filial love for God and of fraternal love towards other people. St. Josemaría considered divine filiation to be the foundation for all the spiritual life of the faithful of Opus Dei.

"Divine filiation," he said, "is the basis of the spirit of Opus Dei. . . . Divine filiation is a joyful truth, a consoling mystery. Divine filiation fills all our spiritual life, because it shows us how to speak to God, to know and to love our Father in heaven. And it makes our interior struggle overflow with hope and gives us the trusting simplicity of little children. More than that: precisely because we are children of God, we can contemplate in

---

2. Ibid.

3. *The Way*, no. 291.

love and wonder everything as coming from the hands of our Father, God the Creator. And so we become contemplatives in the middle of the world, loving the world."[4]

Divine filiation should, in a special way, lead every Christian to realize that "he is grafted onto Christ through baptism . . . and so, like Christ, he has to live for other men, loving each and every one around him and indeed all humanity."[5]

A path of holiness through work and the duties of each day

With Opus Dei, God opened up a practical path for the sanctification of Christians in the world. One specific characteristic of its spirit is the insistence that work can and should be the occasion for seeking holiness and doing apostolate. This includes the entire gamut of family and social duties, cultural and leisure activities, in a word, one's entire daily life.

"We have come to call attention once again to the example of Jesus, who spent thirty years in Nazareth, working as a carpenter. In his hands, a professional occupation, similar to that carried out by millions of people all over the world, was turned into a divine task. It became a part of our Redemption, a way to salvation."[6]

The founder never tired of pointing out that for ordinary Christians "everyday life is the true setting for your lives as Christians." In a homily on October 8, 1967, during a Mass on the campus of the University of Navarra in Spain, he said, "Your ordinary contact with God takes place where your fellow men, your yearnings, your work and your affections are. There you have your daily encounter with Christ. It is in the midst of the

---

4. *Christ Is Passing By*, nos. 64–65.

5. Ibid., no. 106.

6. *Conversations with Monsignor Escrivá*, no. 55.

most material things of the earth that we must sanctify ourselves, serving God and all mankind.

"I have taught this constantly using words from holy Scripture. The world is not evil, because it has come from God's hands, because it is His creation, because *Yahweh looked upon it and saw that it was good* (cf. Gen 1:7 ff.). We ourselves, mankind, make it evil and ugly with our sins and infidelities. Have no doubt: any kind of evasion of the honest realities of daily life is for you, men and women of the world, something opposed to the will of God.

"On the contrary, you must understand now, more clearly, that God is calling you to serve Him *in and from* the ordinary, material and secular activities of human life. He waits for us every day, in the laboratory, in the operating theatre, in the army barracks, in the university chair, in the factory, in the workshop, in the fields, in the home and in all the immense panorama of work. Understand this well: there is something holy, something divine, hidden in the most ordinary situations, and it is up to each one of you to discover it.

"There is no other way. Either we learn to find our Lord in ordinary, everyday life, or else we shall never find Him."[7]

Unity of life

St. Josemaría used to tell his spiritual children that in their lives, there had to come a moment when it wasn't possible to distinguish between prayer and work, because work (which includes other daily duties) must be transformed into prayer.

Someone who does not know the charism of Opus Dei might think it strange to hear the founder saying, as he did on

---

7. "Passionately Loving the World," in *Conversations with Monsignor Escrivá*, nos. 113–123.

many occasions, that a vocation to Opus Dei is essentially contemplative. This is, nevertheless, the ideal of one who is called to seek sanctity in the world: to make daily life into a continuous prayer, an uninterrupted dialogue with God, with this God "who constantly speaks to us through events and through people," and who constantly gives us his love and ask us for love.

Thus St. Josemaría was able to say that the spiritual feature proper to Opus Dei is unity of life. When one makes sanctified and sanctifying work the backbone of the spiritual life, when prayer, mortification and work are directed towards apostolic initiative in the middle of the world—loving one's neighbor (family, colleagues, friends), being of service to them and helping them get closer to God—then the various aspects of Christian life merge and interpenetrate in a harmonious unity. In the simplicity of daily routine, they are like the facets of a diamond reflecting the light of Christian love: love for God and, inseparably, love for neighbor.

As the founder said: "To fulfill the will of God in work, to contemplate God in work, to work for the love of God and one's neighbor, to convert work into a means of apostolate, to give divine value to the human: this is the simple and strong unity of life we must have and must teach others."[8]

These, then, are some of the key characteristics of the spiritual message of Opus Dei.

---

8. Letter of March 11, 1940, no. 14.

APPENDIX II

※

EXCERPTS FROM POPE JOHN PAUL II
AT THE CANONIZATION OF ST. JOSEMARÍA

I. FROM HIS HOMILY DURING THE CANONIZA-TION CEREMONY (ROME, OCTOBER 6, 2002)

" 'The ordinary life of a Christian who has faith,' Josemaría Escrivá used to say, 'when he works or rests, when he prays or sleeps, at all times, is a life in which God is always present.' This supernatural vision of life unfolds an extraordinarily rich horizon of salvific perspectives, because, even in the apparently monotonous flow of normal earthly events, God comes close to us and we can cooperate with his plan of salvation. So it is easier to understand what the Second Vatican Council affirmed: 'there is no question, then, of the Christian message inhibiting men from building up the world . . . on the contrary it is an incentive to do these very things.'

"To elevate the world to God and transform it from within: this is the ideal the holy founder points out to you, dear brothers and sisters, who rejoice today to see him raised to the glory of the altars. He continues to remind you of the need not to let yourselves be frightened by a materialist culture that threatens to dissolve the genuine identity of Christ's disciples. He liked to repeat forcefully that the Christian faith is opposed to conformism and interior inertia.

"Following in his footsteps, spread in society the consciousness that we are all called to holiness whatever our race, class, society or age. In the first place, struggle to be saints yourselves, cultivating an evangelical style of humility and service, abandonment to Providence and of constant listening to the voice of the Spirit. In this way, you will be the *salt of the earth* (cf. Mt 5:13) and *your light so shine before men, that they may see your good works and give glory to your Father who is in heaven* (ibid., 5:16).

"Those who want to serve the cause of the Gospel faithfully will certainly encounter misunderstandings and difficulties. The Lord purifies and shapes all those he calls to follow him with the mysterious power of the Cross; but 'in the Cross,' the new saint repeated, 'we find light, peace and joy: *Lux in Cruce, requies in Cruce, gaudium in Cruce!*' "

II. FROM HIS ADDRESS AFTER THE MASS OF THANKSGIVING FOR THE CANONIZATION (ROME, OCTOBER 7, 2002)

"Saint Josemaría was chosen by the Lord to proclaim the universal call to holiness and to indicate that everyday life, its customary activities, are a path towards holiness. It could be said that he was *the saint of the ordinary*. He was really convinced that, for whoever lives with an outlook of faith, everything offers an opportunity for a meeting with God, everything becomes a stimulus for prayer. Seen in that way, daily life reveals an unsuspected greatness. Holiness is really put on everyone's doorstep.

"Josemaría Escrivá was a saint of great humanity. All those who dealt with him, of whatever level of education or social condition, felt him to be a father, totally dedicated to the service of the others, because he was convinced that each soul is a marvelous treasure; in fact, each person is worth all the Blood of Christ. This attitude of service is plain to see in his dedication to priestly ministry and in the magnanimity with which he pushed ahead so many works of evangelization and of human development to help the poorest.

"The Lord made him understand deeply the gift of our divine filiation. Saint Josemaría taught how to contemplate the tender face of a Father in God, who speaks to us through the most varied vicissitudes of life. A Father who loves us, who follows us step by step and protects us, understands us and waits for a response of love from each one of us. The consideration of this paternal presence, which accompanies him everywhere, gives the Christian an unshakable confidence; at every moment he should confide in the heavenly Father. He never feels alone, nor is he afraid. In the Cross, when it appears, he does not see a punishment but rather a mission entrusted by the Lord himself. The Christian is necessarily optimistic, because he knows that he is a son of God in Christ.

"Saint Josemaría was profoundly convinced that Christian life entails a mission and an apostolate: we are in the world to save it with Christ. He loved the world passionately, with a "redemptive love" (cf. *Catechism of the Catholic Church*, no. 604). It is precisely for this reason that his teachings have helped so many ordinary members of the faithful discover the redemptive power of faith, its capacity to transform the earth.

"This is a message that has abundant and fruitful implications for the evangelizing mission of the Church. It fosters the Christianization of the world 'from within,' showing that there can be no conflict between the divine law and the demands of genuine human progress. This saintly priest taught that Christ must be the apex of all human activity (see Jn 12:32). His message impels the Christian to act in places where the future of society is being shaped. From the laity's active presence in all the professions and at the most advanced frontiers of development, there can only come a positive contribution to the strengthening of that harmony between faith and culture which is one of the great needs of our time."

Excerpts from Cardinal Joseph Ratzinger
(later Pope Benedict XVI)

I. FROM THE HOMILY DURING THE MASS OF THANKSGIVING FOR THE BEATIFICATION OF JOSEMARÍA ESCRIVÁ, FOR GERMAN–SPEAKING FAITHFUL (BASILICA OF THE HOLY APOSTLES, ROME, MAY 19, 1992)

"The desire to see God's will and to identify his will with God's was always the basic motivation of Josemaría Escrivá's life . . . throughout his life, as a fisher of God, he kept throwing out the divine nets tirelessly in the seas of our history, to bring great and small to the light, to return their sight to them. . . .

"The meaning of the word 'holy' has undergone a dangerous narrowing in the course of time, and this certainly still influences it today. It makes us think of the saints whose statues and paintings we see at the altars, of miracles and heroic virtues, and it suggests that holiness is for a few chosen ones, among whom we cannot be included. Then we leave holiness to the few, the unknown number, and content ourselves with being just the way we are. Amidst this spiritual apathy,

Josemaría Escrivá issued a wake-up call, shouting: 'No! Holiness is not something extra, it is what is normal for every baptized person. Holiness does not consist of the sort of heroism that is impossible to imitate, but has a thousand forms and can become a reality anywhere, in any job. It is normal, and it consists of directing one's ordinary life towards God and filling it through with the spirit of faith.'

"Conscious of this message, our new Blessed journeyed untiringly through different continents, speaking to everyone to encourage them to be saints, to live the adventure of being Christians wherever their lives took them. In that way he became a great man of action, who lived by God's will. . . . He dared to be something like a Don Quixote of God. After all, does it not seem quixotic to teach, in the middle of today's world, about humility, obedience, chastity, detachment from material possessions, and forgetfulness of self? God's will was what was really reasonable to him, and that showed that the most seemingly irrational things were really reasonable."

II. TEXT OF AN ARTICLE BY CARDINAL RATZINGER IN *L'OSSERVATORE ROMANO* ON THE DAY OF ST. JOSEMARIÁ'S CANONIZATION (OCTOBER 6, 2002).

I have always been impressed by Josemaría Escrivá's explanation of the name "Opus Dei": an explanation which we might call biographical and which gives us an idea of the founder's spiritual profile. Escrivá knew he had to found something, but he was also conscious that what he was founding was not his own work, that he himself did not invent anything and that the Lord was merely making use of him. So it was not his work, but Opus Dei (God's Work). He was only the instrument for God's action.

In thinking about this, I remember the Lord's words in John's Gospel: "My Father is working still" (Jn 5:17). These are words that Jesus spoke in a discussion with a few experts in religion who did not want to recognize that God can work even on the Sabbath. This is still an ongoing debate, in a certain way, among the men and women—also Christians—of our time. There are those who think that after creation, God "withdrew" and took no further interest in our daily affairs. To this way of thinking, God can no longer enter the fabric of our daily lives. But we have a denial of this in Jesus' words. A man open to God's presence realizes that God is always working and is still working today: we must therefore let him in and let him work. That is how things which give humanity a future and renew it are born.

All this helps us understand why Josemaría Escrivá did not claim to be the "founder" of anything, but only someone who wanted to do God's will and second his action, his work, precisely, God's. In this regard, Escrivá de Balaguer's theocentrism, consistent with Jesus' words, means being confident that God did not withdraw from the world, that God is working today, and that all we have to do is put ourselves at his disposal, make ourselves available to him, and responsive to his call, is an extremely important message. It is a message that helps to overcome what can be considered the great temptation of our time: the claim, that after the "big bang" God withdrew from history, God's action did not stop with the "big bang" but continues in time, both in the world of nature and in the human world.

Thus the founder of the Opus said: "I did not invent anything; another is acting and I am merely ready to serve him as an instrument." This is how the name and the whole reality that we call Opus Dei is profoundly linked with the interior life of the founder who, while remaining very discreet on this point, gives us to understand that he was in a permanent dialogue, a real contact with the One who created us and works for us and with us. The Book of Exodus says of Moses (33:11) "thus the Lord used to speak to Moses as to a friend." It seems to me that even if the veil of discretion may hide many of the details from us, nonetheless from those small references one realizes that the words "speaking as to a friend" can very aptly be applied to Josemaría Escrivá, who opens the doors of the world to let God come in, work and transform all things.

In this light it is also easier to understand what "holiness" and the "universal vocation to holiness" mean. Knowing a little about the history of saints, knowing that in canonization processes their "heroic" virtues are investigated, we almost inevitably slip into an erroneous concept of holiness: "It is not for me," we are inclined to think, "because I do not feel able to achieve heroic virtues: it's too exalted an ideal for me." Holiness then becomes something reserved for the "important" people, whose images we see above the altars, worlds apart indeed from us normal sinners. However, this is an erroneous concept of holiness, a wrong perception which has been corrected—and this seems to me to be the main point—by Josemaría Escrivá.

Heroic virtue does not mean that the saint works out a "gymnastics" of holiness that ordinary people could not tackle. It means, instead, that God's presence is revealed in the life of a person; it is revealed when the person could do nothing by himself or for himself. Perhaps basically, it is a question of terminology because the adjective "heroic" was badly explained. Heroic virtue does not actually mean that someone has done great things by himself, but that situations arise in his life independently of anything he has done: he was simply transparent and available for God's work. Or, in other words, being holy is nothing other than speaking with God as a friend speaks to a friend. That is holiness.

Being holy does not mean being superior to others; indeed, a saint can be very weak and make many blunders in his life. Holiness is profound contact with God, being a friend of God; it is letting the Other act, the One who really can guarantee that the world is good and happy. If therefore St. Josemaría speaks of the common vocation to holiness, it seems to me that he is basically drawing on his own personal experience, not of having done incredible things himself, but of having let God work. Therefore a renewal, a force for good was born in the world even if human weaknesses will always remain. Truly we are all able, we are all called to open ourselves to this friendship with God, not to let go of God's hands, not to give up, turning and returning to the Lord, speaking to him as to a friend, knowing well that the Lord really is the true friend of everyone, even of those who cannot do great things on their own.

All this has enabled me to discern more clearly the profile of Opus Dei, this surprising link between absolute fidelity to the great tradition of the Church and to her faith, with a disarming simplicity and unconditional openness to all the challenges of this world, in the academic world, in the world of work, in the world of economics, etc. Those who have this link with God, those who have this uninterrupted conversation with him, can dare to respond to these challenges and are no longer afraid because those who are in God's hands always fall into God's hands. This is how fear disappears and, instead, the courage is born to respond to the contemporary world.

OTHER RESOURCES FOR ST. JOSEMARÍA

Biographies

Andrés Vázquez de Prada, *The Founder of Opus Dei*:
Vol. I: The Early Years, Princeton, NJ: Scepter Publishers, 2001.
Vol. II: God and Daring, New York: Scepter Publishers, 2003.
Vol. III: The Divine Ways on Earth, New York: Scepter
   Publishers, 2005.

Pilar Urbano: *The Man of Villa Tevere,* New York: Scepter
   Publishers, 2011.

Ana Sastre Gallego: *Tiempo de caminar,* Madrid: Rialp, 1991.

Salvador Bernal: *Monsignor Josemaría Escrivá, A Profile of the
   Founder of Opus Dei,* London: Scepter Publishers, 1977.

François Gondrand: *At God's Pace. Josemaría Escrivá, Founder of
   Opus Dei,* London: Scepter Publishers, 1989.

Other works about St. Josemaría

Alvaro del Portillo: *Immersed in God,* New York: Scepter Publishers, 1996.

Javier Echevarría: *Memoria del Beato Josemaría Escrivá,* Madrid:
   Rialp, 2000.

Pedro Casciaro: *Dream and your Dreams will Fall Short,*
   London: Scepter Publishers, 1998.

Alfonso Balcells: *Memoria ingenua,* Madrid: Rialp, 2009.

Sources on the Internet for St. Josemaría

Complete works: *http://www.escrivaworks.org*
Biography and documentation: *www.josemariaescriva.info*
YouTube: *http://www.youtube.com/josemariaescriva*